Louis Riel

with profiles of
Gabriel Dumont
and Poundmaker

World Book, Inc.
a Scott Fetzer company
Chicago

BIOGRAPHICAL ⊕ CONNECTIONS

Writer: Robert Knight.

World Book, Inc.
233 N. Michigan Ave.
Chicago, IL 60601

For information about other World Book publications, visit our Web site at **www.worldbook.com** or call **1-800-WORLDBK (967-5325)**.
For information about sales to schools and libraries, call **1-800-975-3250** (**United States**), or **1-800-837-5365** (**Canada**).

Library of Congress Cataloging-in-Publication Data

Knight, Robert.
   Louis Riel with profiles of Gabriel Dumont and Poundmaker / [writer, Robert Knight].
      p. cm. -- (Biographical connections)
   Summary: "A biography of Louis Riel, a Métis leader who, in the 1800's, sought better treatment of his people by the Canadian establishment. Also profiled are two prominent individuals, who are associated through the influences they had on one another, the successes they achieved, or the goals they worked toward. Includes recommended readings and web sites"--Provided by publisher.
   Includes bibliographical references and index.
   ISBN-13: 978-0-7166-1824-9
   ISBN-10: 0-7166-1824-9
   1. Riel, Louis, 1844-1885. 2. Métis--Biography. 3. Dumont, Gabriel, 1838-1906. 4. Poundmaker, 1842-1886. 5. Riel Rebellion, 1885. I. World Book, Inc. II. Series.
E99.M47R45 2007
971.05'1092--dc22
[B]
                                        2006015547

Printed in the United States of America
1 2 3 4 5 10 09 08 07 06

Contents

Acknowledgments

The publisher gratefully acknowledges the following sources for the photographs in this volume. All maps are the exclusive property of World Book, Inc.

Cover Glenbow Museum NA-504-3;
O. B. Buell Library and Archives Canada;
Glenbow Museum PA-2218-1

6 WORLD BOOK map
7 Glenbow Museum PA-2218-1
9 WORLD BOOK map
15 © Corbis/Bettmann
23 Mary Evans Picture Library
27 Library of Congress
29 Granger Collection
32 Glenbow Museum NA-1406-55
34 Glenbow Museum NA-1269-21
35 Glenbow Museum NA-3694-1
45 Glenbow Museum NA-1039-1
48 Glenbow Museum NA-20-8
64 Glenbow Museum NA-1313-2
69 Glenbow Museum NA-682-6
78 Glenbow Museum NA-1480-40
85 Bridgeman Art Library
88 AP/WideWorld
89 O. B. Buell, Library and Archives Canada/C-001875
90 WORLD BOOK map
93 Glenbow Museum NA-1344-2
94 Glenbow Museum NA-1241-10
99 Glenbow Museum NA-1479-1
103 Glenbow Museum NA-1353-6
105 Glenbow Museum NA-363-63

Preface

Biographical Connections takes a contextual approach in presenting the lives of important people. In each volume, there is a biography of a central figure. This biography is preceded and followed by profiles of other individuals whose lifework connects in some way to that of the central figure. The three subjects are associated through the influences they had on one another, the successes they achieved, or the goals they worked toward. The series includes men and women from around the world and throughout history in a variety of fields.

This volume examines the lives of three extraordinary individuals who lived on the western plains (what we now call the Prairie Provinces) of Canada during the 1800's. Louis Riel, Gabriel Dumont, and Poundmaker each witnessed the epochal transformation that was occurring in the plains ecology, ways of life, and culture, and they acted out their roles on the stage of that remarkable drama.

Louis Riel, the central biography in this volume, tried to forge a national identity for his *Métis* (people of mixed Indian and European blood) who might then claim their true place in the Canadian confederation. Gabriel Dumont, the subject of the first profile in this volume, also a Métis, tried to obtain better governance and fairer treatment for the Métis people from the Canadian establishment. Poundmaker, the subject of the volume's last profile, was a Cree Indian with Métis blood. He sought to prepare his people for the impending changes he could foresee and to forge a political consciousness among all the various Indian tribes of western Canada.

Of these three men, Riel, the instigator of rebellions, casts the longest shadow across Canada's collective consciousness. Even today, some Canadians struggle to understand Riel's significance and argue over the role he played in Canada's national drama. The profile of Poundmaker illustrates the strivings of a remarkable Indian leader to come to terms with a world and culture dominated increasingly by nonnative peoples. Finally, Gabriel

Dumont's profile portrays a western folk hero who was tragically sidelined by the march of technology and modernity.

Each man, in some measure, succeeded; in many particulars, each man failed. Nonetheless, the amalgamation of people, places, and cultures that we today call "Canada" owes at least a piece of its identity to these men of the plains and their lives' work. ■

Louis Riel, Gabriel Dumont, and Poundmaker lived on the western plains of Canada during the 1800's in what we now call the Prairie Provinces: Alberta, Saskatchewan, and Manitoba.

Gabriel Dumont (1837–1906)

Gabriel Dumont was a Métis leader of Canada's Saskatchewan plains during the second half of the 1800's. The Métis *(may TEES* or *may TEE)* are people of mixed European and Indian blood. Dumont achieved his greatest fame commanding a Métis and Indian army in the 1885 conflict that came to be known as the North West Rebellion. Led by Louis Riel, the rebellion was, in part, an attempt by the local Métis—and some Indian— populations to gain rights of self-government and other considerations from the Canadian government in Ottawa.

Dumont achieved initial successes on the battlefield with his small, poorly equipped army against much larger forces fielded by the Canadian government. These successes are due, many historians have judged, to Dumont's exceptional talents as a commander in guerrilla-style warfare.

Dumont also exemplified a plains Métis lifestyle that was rendered obsolete during his own lifetime by rapid settlement of the west, transformation of the plains environment into a region of intensive agriculture, and the railroad and other industrial technologies.

In his own element—the western prairies before the coming of the railroad and massive settlement—Dumont was virtually unequaled as a hunter, guide, horseman, and marksman. In many respects, he was an authentic hero of the Old West.

COUREURS DE BOIS

France had colonized much of northern North America, beginning in the 1500's. By the 1600's this region became known as New France. Although the French established farming communities in the St. Lawrence Valley, in present-day Quebec, many of the people of New France were engaged in the trading and export of furs.

These French fur traders, called *coureurs de bois (koor RUR duh BWAH)*—literally, "runners of the woods"—penetrated the immense hinterlands of North America, far beyond the settled farming communities of the St. Lawrence Valley. They established a string of trading posts between what is now the city of Montreal and the province of Saskatchewan, on the high interior plains. The coureurs also ranged south and southwest into areas that are now part of the United States. Closely associated with the coureurs de bois were *voyageurs*, people who transported goods, especially furs, across long distances on foot or by means of canoes. The voyageurs also had licenses to trade in furs while the coureurs de bois traded illegally.

To make fur-trading a successful enterprise, the coureurs de bois and voyageurs developed peaceful and trusting relations with the Indian communities scattered across woodland North America. Often, they cemented such bonds through marriage with Indian women. Generations of their Métis descendants would populate much of French Canada.

In the Red River settlement and elsewhere, the French Métis largely retained French language and culture, including Roman Catholicism. Some spoke a hybrid language called *Michif (MEE cheef)*, derived from French and the language of the Cree Indians, but most Michif-speakers also knew French. In other respects, the Métis way of life was not unlike that of the surrounding Indian peoples to whom they were related. Like the Indians, they favored hunting over farming, and many lived a seminomadic lifestyle, settling in one place only for the winter.

THE DUMONT FAMILY

Gabriel Dumont was born in December 1837 in the Red River settlement, a region that would eventually become the Canadian province of Manitoba. At that time, the immense tract of land that today makes up much of western and northern Canada was known as "Rupert's Land." The Red River settlement lay in the southeastern part of Rupert's Land.

The Dumont family were French Métis, mainly descendants of French fur traders and Indian women. In the 1800's, communities of

French Métis were scattered across western Canada— Rupert's Land—but an especially large concentration lived in the Red River settlement. Living in their midst were some Scottish and English Métis, but the French were by far the most numerous of the Métis peoples, such that the term Métis has often been taken to mean people of French and Indian origin.

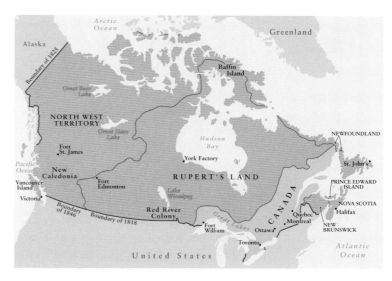

Members of the Dumont clan descended from Jean-Baptiste Dumont, a French voyageur, and a Sarcee Indian woman whose name is unknown. Together Jean-Baptiste and the Sarcee woman had three boys. The child Isidore was Gabriel Dumont's father.

In his fur-trading activities, Jean-Baptiste Dumont, Gabriel's grandfather, probably ranged between Montreal (in present-day Quebec) in the east and Fort Edmonton (Edmonton, in present-day Alberta) in the west. He gathered furs for, and received payment from, officials of the Hudson's Bay Company (HBC). The British-based company owned the vast area known as Rupert's Land and ran it so as to maximize profits for company investors, very few of whom lived in North America.

By about 1800, Jean-Baptiste and his family were living near Fort Edmonton in the North Saskatchewan River Valley. This was shortgrass prairie country of the relatively dry high interior plains of northern North America. Wide stretches of grassland were broken by isolated stands of aspens and birch, as well as rare outcroppings of rugged, hilly terrain such as the Cypress Hills to the south. The rich ecosystem supported deer, pronghorns, rabbits, coyotes, and all kinds of burrowing creatures, such as prairie dogs, badgers, and ground squirrels. Rivers and scattered lakes and ponds of glacial

Dumont was born in 1837 in the Red River settlement, a region that would eventually become the Canadian province of Manitoba. The Red River settlement lay in the southeastern part of Rupert's Land, an immense tract of land that today makes up much of western and northern Canada.

origin teemed with fish and supported great numbers of water fowl. Beyond all of these riches, however, the land harbored immense herds of American buffalo (bison). According to some estimates, as many as 20 million buffalo roamed the interior plains of North America at one time, but their numbers went into rapid decline after 1850.

The buffalo were the mainstay of the people of the Canadian plains, both Indian and Métis. This vital and irreplaceable resource would virtually disappear during Dumont's lifetime.

GABRIEL DUMONT'S EARLY LIFE

In 1833, Isidore Dumont, Gabriel's father, married a Métis woman named Louise Laframboise. Possibly because Isidore's two older brothers were already well established in the Fort Edmonton community, he and Louise struck out on their own, moving to the Red River settlement, roughly 750 miles (about 1,200 kilometers) to the east.

Isidore cleared three acres (1.2 hectares) of land along the Red River in the Métis community of St. Boniface to make a farm for the growing Dumont family. The farm was typical of Métis landholding patterns, a legacy of ancient French custom. The Métis occupied narrow strips of land along rivers and streams. Inland from the river frontage were commons where the farmers communally held pasturing rights. Few of the Métis held formal deeds to their land, a factor that would greatly complicate land surveys when settlers from the east began arriving in large numbers in the last quarter of the 1800's.

The Dumont family, like their Métis neighbors, lived simply. They inhabited a mud plaster log house. A barn, several Red River carts—simple two-wheeled wagons—and some canoes on the Dumont property gave evidence of a fairly prosperous existence. The family heavily supplemented the fruits of their tiny farm with fish and game. Skill with a rifle was part and parcel of Métis coming of age.

BUFFALO HUNTS

When Dumont was a young boy, the buffalo were still relatively plentiful on the western plains. Buffalo meat was a staple of the diet of most Métis, and large, highly organized, weeks-long buffalo hunts were an integral part of Métis social and cultural life, as well as an opportunity to train the young in plains survival skills.

In the summer of 1840, when Dumont was a toddler not yet 3 years old, a large Métis hunting party from the Red River settlement carried out a two-month buffalo hunt that amply provisioned the participants for the coming winter. Dumont's family was among the group, his father, Isidore, being a good shot and capable organizer.

The hunting party consisted of over 1,600 people, 1,210 Red River carts, 400 horses, and 500 dogs. On the trail, the procession stretched out 5 miles (8 kilometers). Sentries kept watch at night for bands of Sioux Indians, the traditional enemies of the Métis. Other scouts fanned out in advance of the party in order to find the buffalo herds.

Once a herd was sighted, hundreds of mounted Métis hunters converged on the bolting beasts, rifles ablaze. The best marksmen among them could bring down a dozen buffalo per day. After the kill, the hard work of butchering it and processing the meat and hides would begin, supervised and mainly carried out by the women.

At the end of the 1840 buffalo hunt, the Métis party returned with about 500 tons (450 metric tones) of preserved (dried) buffalo meat. Isidore Dumont himself brought home about 3,500 pounds (1,575 kilograms).

Sometime in the early 1840's, Isidore Dumont moved his family back to the Saskatchewan River country to the west. They settled near Fort Pitt on the North Saskatchewan River near the present-day border between Saskatchewan and Alberta. Isidore's motivation may have been to move closer to the buffalo herds and trade in buffalo hides, which was becoming more and more lucrative.

In 1848, when Gabriel was about 10 years old, the Dumont family moved back to the Red River settlement. During this journey, young Gabriel bravely warned the traveling party of the approach of hostile Sioux warriors and requested a rifle to help defend the small Métis party. The "warriors" turned out to be a herd of buffalo, but his uncle was so proud of his nephew that he gave Gabriel his own rifle, which the boy named *"le petit,"* meaning "the little one" in

French. Thereafter, throughout his life, Gabriel Dumont always called his favorite rifle "le petit."

The family now made their home in White Horse Plain (today called St. François Xavier), a settlement to the west of Fort Garry (present-day Winnipeg). Isidore and his family soon became well integrated into the buffalo-hunting Métis community.

GABRIEL DUMONT COMES OF AGE

In 1851, an event occurred that was to pass into Métis legend and also marked effective passage into adulthood for the 13-year-old Dumont. That summer, a buffalo hunting party of over 300 Métis men, women, and children departed from White Horse Plain for the open prairies to the south and west. In the party were the Dumonts, including Gabriel, now an able rider and handler of horses and an accurate shot.

On July 13, the Métis party were camped near a land formation called the Grand Coteau *(KOH TOH)*, a long, low butte (steep-sided hill) stretching from Turtle Mountain near the southwest corner of present-day Manitoba southeastward into Dakota country (now North Dakota). Suddenly, a large war party of about 2,000 Sioux appeared on the high ground above the camp. The Sioux were likely contesting the presence of the Métis hunting party on territory the Indians considered theirs.

The Métis leaders realized they were about to be attacked by the Sioux with their great numerical superiority. They quickly made a temporary fortification by gathering their Red River carts into a tight ring, axle to axle, and placed the women, children, and animals inside. Then, they dug pits in the ground in front of the carts to give the Métis sharpshooters unimpeded sight lines and protect the women, children, and animals from the Indians' fire.

The Sioux attack came fast and furious, raining bullets and arrows on the Métis formation. Amazingly, fewer than 80 Métis shooters, among them the teen-aged Dumont, held off the enormous Sioux war party, which eventually withdrew. But the next day, July 14, the Sioux party returned to exact vengeance. Once again, the Métis leaders quickly organized their mobile fortification with the carts and prepared for battle. That second day of battle lasted five hours. Finally, the Sioux withdrew, beaten for good. Although no one knows how many Sioux died in the Battle of the Grand Coteau, as the action came to be called, many historians believe that perhaps 80 Sioux warriors were killed in the battle. Only one member of the Métis party was lost, a scout who was unable to reach the relative safety of the cart fortification. Stories of the heroism of the Métis hunting party at Grand Coteau would be passed down to generations of Métis children.

DUMONT THE ENTREPRENEUR

In 1858, Dumont's mother died. That same year, Dumont married Madeleine Wilkie, the Métis daughter of a Scottish trader. By all accounts, their marriage was a happy one. They had no children of their own but adopted a girl, named Annie, and a boy named Alexis, a relative of Dumont's.

Sometime in the late 1850's or early 1860's, the Dumonts moved back to the Saskatchewan country, settling in the vicinity of Fort Carlton, a trading post on the North Saskatchewan River near the forks of the North and South Saskatchewan rivers. In 1863, Dumont was elected chief of an annual Métis buffalo hunt originating in the Fort Carlton area. Around 1868, Dumont's family settled near the village of Batoche *(buh TAHSH)*, another river community, about 20 miles (32 kilometers) east of Fort Carlton. In 1870, possession of the western plains and the vast lands to the north passed from the Hudson's Bay Company to the Canadian government. To administer it, Canada assembled the vast region into the North West Territories (later known as the Northwest Territories). At the same time, the federal government in Ottawa created the province of Manitoba in the Red River Valley.

Soon thereafter, the population of the Saskatchewan country in the Northwest Territories began to grow as Métis from Manitoba began to pull up stakes and migrate westward out of that newly formed province, and small numbers of white settlers from the east began arriving. Seeing opportunity in these changes, Dumont started a ferry across the South Saskatchewan River a few miles (or kilometers) north of Batoche to accommodate traffic on the Carlton Trail.

That important trail linked Fort Edmonton in the west with Fort Garry (now part of Winnipeg, Manitoba) in the east. Dumont eventually opened a store and built a house for his family on the east side of the ferry. The little settlement associated with the ferry became known as "Gabriel's Crossing."

In addition to their income from the ferry and the store, the Dumont family derived a comfortable living through farming, hunting, and fishing. Neighbors could, perhaps enviously, judge the Dumonts' relative prosperity by the slate billiard table that Dumont purchased for the store and the hand-cranked washing machine that helped ease Madeleine's domestic burdens in the Dumont home.

LEADER OF THE COMMUNITY

In 1873, Dumont helped establish a local government for the community of St. Laurent, a few miles (or kilometers) north of Gabriel's Crossing. Dumont and several other community leaders formed a council of eight, electing Dumont as president. The council enacted a brief legal code, asserted its right to levy taxes, and declared its loyalty to the Dominion of Canada. The St. Laurent Council was the first local government to be established in Canada between Manitoba and the Rocky Mountains.

Dumont was again elected president of the St. Laurent Council in December 1874. However, the promising experiment in local government was soon to be abandoned. Lawrence Clarke, a government official at nearby Fort Carlton, wrote to Lieutenant Governor Alexander Morris, the chief executive in the Northwest Territories, in early 1875 expressing suspicions that the St. Laurent council members had established a "provisional government" and were in open revolt against properly constituted Canadian authority. Morris responded by sending a North West Mounted Police (NWMP) patrol to St. Laurent to investigate the situation there. The police reported back to the lieutenant governor that Clarke's suspicions were without any foundation. However, the intrusion of the North West Mounted Police into the St. Laurent community apparently intimidated the council members to the extent that they ceased enforcing the council's authority, and the whole enterprise folded.

Nevertheless, the lack of well-established local and other governmental structures in the Northwest Territories, the federal entity that now administered the Saskatchewan country, created a vacuum that was to become more and more problematic. To fill the vacuum, natural leaders such as Dumont began organizing their neighbors to petition the federal government in Ottawa for much-needed services and reforms. In 1877 and also in 1878, Dumont chaired meetings among Métis leading citizens that formulated such petitions, subsequently presented to the federal government.

In 1880, Dumont protested a proposal from the territorial government to charge a fee for cutting wood on Crown (public) lands. Dumont successfully petitioned the government to drop the plan. Dumont and his Métis associates and neighbors again petitioned the federal government on a variety of important topics in 1881.

At the heart of the Métis's petitions was concern about land. Most of the Métis people in the Saskatchewan country had taken possession of their land by virtue of living on it for a period of time. There were few titles (legal documents showing the right to possession of property) or land registrations. As new settlers—especially whites from the East—filtered in, Métis residents began to worry

Gabriel Dumont served as military leader of the North West Rebellion, a revolt against the Canadian government in 1885. He helped Louis Riel lead the Métis (persons of mixed white and American Indian ancestry) in a fight for land rights. Dumont is shown in this sketch drilling a company of Métis soldiers who would take part in the rebellion.

that they might be evicted from their lands. Beyond the issue of land tenure itself, however, there was the issue of Métis landholding patterns. The Métis residents of the Saskatchewan country knew that when federal surveyors had come to Manitoba, they had measured off square lots. But the settled Métis in the Saskatchewan River Valley (as in the Red River Valley) had occupied strips along rivers, in the traditional French pattern. They wanted to make sure that future surveyors—certain to arrive, sooner or later—would respect these holdings.

Other concerns received representation in the Métis petitions as well. The more forward-thinking among the Métis realized that changes afoot in the territory would require the Métis people to settle down in more permanent patterns than in previous generations. They asked for help from the federal government to learn farming and establish schools.

THE TERRITORIAL GOVERNMENT

In the 1870's and 1880's, the Canadian Northwest Territories included the Saskatchewan country and much of the land now identified as western and northern Canada. The executive head of the territorial government during this period was Edgar Dewdney, the Ottawa-appointed lieutenant governor and Indian commissioner (person who makes treaties with Indians). In the late 1870's and early 1880's, the territorial capital was at Battleford, a village at the fork of the North Saskatchewan and Battle rivers and west of Fort Carlton. Canadian officials in 1882 moved the territorial capital far to the south, to Regina, now a fast-growing settlement by virtue of its position on the Canadian Pacific Railway.

In 1882, the Canadian federal government reorganized the Northwest Territories, creating four administrative districts: the District of Assiniboia, the District of Saskatchewan, the District of Athabaska, and the District of Alberta. Each district ranged westward from the Manitoba region to the eastern border of British Columbia.

The 1882 reorganization of the territory did little, however, to improve governance or to address grievances such as those Dumont and his associates had itemized repeatedly in their petitions to the federal government. By this time, moreover, other forces at work in the territory were sowing seeds of dissatisfaction among its inhabitants.

DESPERATE CONDITIONS

Several features of the natural environment were now working against the welfare of many inhabitants of the Saskatchewan country. First and foremost, the buffalo herds on which Indians and Métis especially had depended, were virtually gone. The collapse of the plains buffalo population in North America in the 1870's and 1880's was the result both of the spread of European-style settlement, with its intensive agriculture and—most notoriously—indiscriminate killing by nonnative hunters. It was an unparalleled catastrophe for the Indian nations of the northern plains—Cree, Assiniboines, Blackfoot, and others—and for many of the Métis inhabitants as well.

Crop failures plagued the region, too, as seasonal rains failed in a cyclical turn towards drought. The drought conditions hurt everyone—white settlers trying to scratch out a living from the soil, as well as Indians and Métis families trying to adjust to settled life and learn farming. Farming in a marginal climate is difficult, and the full development of agriculture in the drier, western reaches of the plains would await dry farming techniques, introduced a few decades later.

From 1880 on, desperate conditions afflicted Indians and many Métis in the Saskatchewan country, who without ample supplies of preserved buffalo meat, endured "starving times" each winter season. To make matters worse, other game became scarcer with the prevailing dry conditions and overhunting.

At the same time, the inhabitants of the region witnessed a growing influx of settlers from the east, aided greatly by the extension of the railroad westward to Regina (Saskatchewan) in 1882, and to Calgary (Alberta) in 1883. Métis concerns about the validity of their land tenure now loomed large. Such concerns were only intensified when stories of Métis families evicted from their lands by new settlers, armed with survey-confirmed land deeds, circulated.

Dumont heard one such story in the early 1880's, which he recounted years later in his memoirs. A group of about 30 Métis families were pushed off their land by new settlers at Fort Edmonton, so the story went. When the Métis appealed to the police, they were told that the dispossession was legal, and nothing could be done. Whether the story is true, it certainly raised tensions in the mid-Saskatchewan region, and the pattern of dispossession of Métis was by no means unprecedented in the Northwest Territories.

THE MÉTIS LEADERS TURN TO RIEL

Frustrated with the federal government's inaction in the face of the growing crisis in the Saskatchewan country, Dumont called a meeting of Métis leaders in the Batoche region in March 1884. The participants rehashed grievances and concluded that a larger meeting with representatives from the entire Métis community in the central Saskatchewan region should be convened as soon as possible. On April 28, 1884, several hundred regional Métis leaders gathered and selected a six-member committee to catalog grievances and to seek out support from non-Métis communities in the region. One of those six committee members was Dumont.

Dumont and the other five committee members, acknowledging that all previous petitioning efforts had been unproductive, decided to make contact with Riel, known to be living in Montana Territory to the south. Virtually all Métis people in North America knew how Riel had in 1870 attained provincial status for Manitoba on a basis that was highly favorable to the Métis community there. Indeed, Riel had acquired near-mythic status, and there was no reason to doubt that he could achieve for the Saskatchewan Métis what he had done in Manitoba.

Accordingly, the Dumont committee on May 6, 1884, drew up a resolution, appending it to a draft list of their grievances:

> We the French and English natives of the North West, knowing that Louis Riel made a bargain with the Government of Canada in 1870, which said bargain is contained mostly in what is known as the "Manitoba Act," have thought it advisable that a delegation be sent to the said Louis Riel, and have his assistance to bring all matters referred to in the above resolutions in a proper shape and form before the Government of Canada, so that our just demands be granted.[1]

On June 4, 1884, Riel was called out of church to meet four men who were asking for him. They were Dumont, Moise Ouellette, Michel Dumas, and James Isbister, all members of the Saskatchewan delegation.

Riel talked to the men and said he would give them an answer to their invitation after a night's sleep. The next morning he told them: "It has been fifteen years since I gave my heart to my country. I am ready to give it again now, but I cannot leave my little family. If you can arrange for them to come I will go with you."[2] The Saskatchewan men answered that they had plenty of room in their wagons and would be glad to take the family of four.

On June 10, 1884, the traveling party, including the four Saskatchewan men and Louis and Marguerite Riel with their two children and meager belongings—all bundled into Red River carts—started their long trip northward to the middle Saskatchewan River Valley. The journey would cover roughly 700 miles (1,120 kilometers), much of it through stretches of remote, rugged territory.

POLITICAL ACTION

The Riel party arrived at Dumont's farm near Batoche on July 5. Eventually, the Riels would be lodged at the home of Charles Nolin, a Riel relative, in Batoche.

Soon after Riel's arrival, Dumont and the other Métis leaders arranged a series of public meetings for Riel to address. On July 8, he addressed a Métis audience in Batoche, his first public address in Canada since 1870. Next, there was a large meeting at Red Deer Hill on July 11. There, several hundred people, mainly English speakers, heard Riel's speech, given in English. On July 19, he spoke to a large audience at Prince Albert, a growing trading town north of Batoche on the North Saskatchewan River. In these early meetings, Riel urged moderation, advocating further petitioning of the federal government for redress of grievances.

During the summer and fall months of 1884, Riel and his Métis associates scored some successes in broadening the base of their movement to include non-French speakers. Most notably, Riel formed an alliance with William Jackson, the head of the Settler's

Union, an association of mainly white farmers that engaged in political agitation for government policies more favorable to small farmers in the territory. Riel and Jackson mutually drafted a revised petition, inclusive of the concerns of the various communities in the mid-Saskatchewan region, which would ultimately be submitted to the federal government.

The Métis under Riel's leadership also tried to reach out politically to the various Indian tribes in the region. These efforts proved disappointing, however; even the more forward-looking Indian chiefs, such as the Cree chief Poundmaker, had very limited success motivating their people to organize politically. During this period of intense political activity, Dumont remained mainly on the sidelines, attending to his own business affairs. However, he stayed in close contact with Riel and was at all times aware of the political situation.

THE PETITION

In December 1884, Riel and Jackson completed work on a new petition, a comprehensive catalog of grievances among the various middle Saskatchewan communities. One section advocated confirming land titles to all squatters, an issue of great interest to the Métis people. Another cited poverty and famine among the Indians and called for substantial increases in government rations. Yet another section recommended the construction of a railroad north to Hudson Bay. This proposal had been put forward by the Settlers' Union and other communities of white farmers who wanted greater competition among railroads to force companies to lower their carrying rates.

Above all else, the petition advocated full provincial status for the region, as the province of Saskatchewan. That was the surest way to protect citizens' rights, the petitioners reasoned, because it would guarantee full representation in the national government.

On Dec. 16, 1884, the completed petition was dispatched to Prime Minister John Macdonald's Cabinet in Ottawa. Soon afterward, receipt of the petition in Ottawa was acknowledged by the federal secretary of state, Adolphe Chapleau. Jackson took the prompt acknowledgment as a sign that the petition would, this time, be heeded.

MÉTIS REBELLION

The petitioners' early optimism, however, turned to disappointment, bitterness, and anger as the winter dragged on with no further response from Ottawa. Some time in February 1885, Riel began to wonder out loud about the possibility of taking up arms against the government. According to Dumont's memoirs, Riel stated, "They [the federal government] should at least answer us, either yes or no. And they cannot say no, since we are only asking for what has already been promised. If they don't give us our rights, we will have to rebel again."[3]

At a secret meeting on March 5, 1885, 11 of Riel's inner circle took an oath that they would use arms if necessary to further their political aims. Dumont was one of the oath takers as were four Dumont relatives.

Apparently at around this time, Riel asked Dumont to gather fighters to form a Métis army. Accordingly, Dumont busied himself recruiting among the Métis of the region and also among neighboring Cree bands. Within two weeks, he had about 300 fighters, mostly Métis but with a few Indians also, under his command, gathered in and around Batoche.

THE PROVISIONAL GOVERNMENT

On March 18, a rumor reached Batoche that a large force of NWMP was approaching. The impending threat spurred the Métis leaders to action. Dumont arrested the local Indian agent, John Lash. According to his memoirs, Dumont stated, "Now when I see a government man, I will take him prisoner . . . . The moment we took up arms, we were in rebellion, and this is not too much."[4] Fighters under Dumont's command raided stores in Batoche for supplies and ammunition, and prepared for imminent action.

The next day, March 19, 1885, Riel proclaimed a provisional government with Pierre Parenteau as president. Riel was never officially part of the provisional government, but was the unofficial leader. He formed a council of advisers called the *Exovedate,* a coined word derived from Latin and meaning "chosen out of the flock." Riel, Dumont, and the other members of the Exovedate council would run the affairs and supervise the defense of the provisional government.

The provisional government was a direct provocation to the authorities in Ottawa, who were being kept up to date on the situation in Saskatchewan District by local government officials and NWMP officials. Macdonald's government responded swiftly. Macdonald appointed Major-General Frederick Middleton as commander of government forces in the Northwest Territories. Arrangements were made to transport several thousand troops rapidly westward by rail to reinforce NWMP forces already on the ground in the territory.

CLASH OF ARMS

The provisional government was about to come under attack. As a defensive measure, Dumont and Riel on March 25 led a Métis force to Duck Lake, a trading village a few miles (or kilometers) west of Batoche. Duck Lake held a strategic position: it was on the Carlton Trail between Batoche and Fort Carlton, from which government troops, according to scouts' reports, were approaching.

On March 26, an improvised government force consisting mainly of NWMP personnel under the command of NWMP superintendent Leif Crozier approached Duck Lake. The large "army" fell far short of the implied threat, comprising only about 100 men. Fighting broke out between Dumont's fighters and the NWMP forces, and a heated battle ensued. The Métis were well placed defensively and overpowered the government force, which retreated after suffering many casualties.

Bad luck had hampered Crozier's force from the start. By improperly loading the cannon the troops had with them, they rendered it useless for the duration of the battle.

The Métis army had taken some casualties, too. Dumont himself was wounded when a bullet grazed the top of his head, "making a furrow," as he said, and causing blood to spurt out. When one of Dumont's fighters saw the blood, he exclaimed, "Oh no—they got you!" Dumont, not too seriously wounded and ready with a quip, replied: "When you don't lose your head, you're not dead."[5]

MIDDLETON'S ARMY ARRIVES

By mid-April 1885, General Middleton's army was advancing on Batoche from the south with a force of 800 soldiers. Dumont prepared to make a stand at Fish Creek, south of Batoche. As at Duck Lake, the Métis general selected his positions wisely. He posted his fighters in a wooded *coulee* (gulch) made by the creek's course. He then cleverly drew Middleton's soldiers into the coulee, where the Métis fighters could take great advantage of their cover and superior positions.

In the Battle of Fish Creek on April 24, 1885, the outnumbered rebel force of 150 Métis and Indians managed to hold the ground and stop Middleton's advance. The battle revealed Dumont's great strengths as a commander in conditions of guerrilla warfare. When at the height of the battle Dumont realized that his fighters were nearly out of ammunition, he had his men set fire to the brush in front of them. The fire and smoke temporarily screened off Dumont's band of fighters from Middleton's soldiers. Dumont had his men whoop and yell to create in impression of imminent threat from a large body of fighters. When the fire died down and the smoke began to clear, Middleton's troops were in retreat.

Fighting between the Métis and Canadian forces ended in May 1885, after Dumont's defeat at Batoche.

INDIANS UNDER ARMS

News of the creation of the Métis provisional government and the Métis victory at Duck Lake in late March spread rapidly. In response, some of the Indian bands in the Saskatchewan Valley took up arms against the government. The Indians in the region had suffered grievous neglect by the federal government in recent years, a period in which many had suffered or died from starvation. Now, years of simmering resentment and anger found an outlet in arms. Small bands of warriors attacked at scattered locations across the region, resulting in several killing sprees.

However, one Indian action, entirely defensive in nature, particularly merited the name of battle. On May 1, Lieutenant-Colonel William Otter, one of Middleton's officers, led a well-equipped force of 300 men out of the town of Battleford toward the Cut Knife Reserve, home of the Poundmaker band. Otter intended to punish the band for their pillaging of Battleford a month earlier. The column approached the Indian camp early on the morning of May 2, giving the Indians only time enough to send their women and children into hiding in the surrounding brush and to take up defensive positions. A six- or seven-hour battle ensued, during which Poundmaker's warriors inflicted serious casualties on the government troops, despite Otter's possession of two cannons and a Gatling gun (an early machine gun). Finally, Otter had enough and withdrew.

Poundmaker's stunning victory would make little difference in the end. After the battle at Cut Knife Reserve, Poundmaker's warriors marched east to join up with Riel's forces at Batoche. By then, they were too late.

The failure of Indians and Métis to form a united front during the brief war that was to become known as the North West Rebellion seriously hobbled the Métis provisional government from the start. Had they established a unified purpose and command, Middleton would have confronted a much more daunting situation in Saskatchewan.

THE BATTLE FOR BATOCHE

Concurrently, Middleton, still camped south of Batoche, was collecting fresh troops and supplies and preparing for a decisive assault on the Métis capital and stronghold. Finally, on May 9, he judged that his well-equipped army of more than 800 troops was ready for action, and he led them northward toward the village.

Meanwhile, Dumont had been preparing the defenses of the village. He and his men dug foxholes—pits big enough to hold three men, at about 75-yard (69-meter) intervals around the town's perimeter. By the time Middleton's troops arrived, the Métis fighters were well-placed for defense, now something of a hallmark of Dumont's generalship.

The battle raged intermittently for three days, with the desperately outnumbered Métis defenders fighting ferociously. At one point during the heat of battle, Dumont asked a grievously wounded comrade, "Are you dead or alive?" to which the man replied: "I won't last much longer." Dumont responded, "Then it is good to want to fight on. You might get two deaths instead of one."[6]

In the end, the Métis fighters' ammunition ran out. On May 12, Dumont, Riel, and the rest of the Métis rebels scattered into the woods and brush around Batoche. Middleton was now in firm control of Batoche; the rebellion was finished.

ESCAPE

Gabriel Dumont had no intention of surrendering to Middleton, as Riel subsequently did on May 15, or of letting himself be caught by Middleton's patrols. Dumont was supremely in his element—the land of the Saskatchewan country—and he was not likely to make any foolish mistakes. Back at Batoche, a priest questioned about Dumont's whereabouts responded, "You are looking for Gabriel? Well, you are wasting your time, there isn't a blade of grass on the prairie he does not know."[7]

Nor was it likely that Dumont would give himself up from desperate hunger. On his first night on the run, the savvy Métis made a beeline for a hidden Sioux lodge and obtained a feast of dried meat for himself and several who were traveling with him.

After 11 days of traveling on horse and by foot and evading government patrols, Dumont reached the border in the company of Michel Dumas, a fellow Métis fugitive. The two men were promptly arrested by U.S. army officers but then released on orders of President Grover Cleveland. By May 29, he was at liberty in the United States.

Dumont, eventually joined by his wife, settled among the Métis in Montana. Madeleine died, probably of tuberculosis, in the spring of 1886. Now, Dumont had little incentive to put down roots in Montana. He reconsidered an invitation he had received from William Cody—"Buffalo Bill"—to join Buffalo Bill's Wild West Show. In June 1886, Dumont informed Cody that he would accept his invitation.

LIFE ON THE ROAD

Dumont traveled by rail, probably for the first time in his life, to Philadelphia in July 1886 to join Buffalo Bill's Wild West Show. He would perform with the show, off and on, for the next three seasons.

Buffalo Bill's Wild West Show was an immensely popular touring show, the creation of frontiersman/showman Cody, that specialized in acts purporting to represent life in the American West. Cody billed Dumont as the "Hero of the Halfbreed Rebellion." Dumont showed off his superb marksmanship with his famous rifle, "le petit," and competed in shooting matches with the legendary Annie Oakley.

While living in the East and touring with Buffalo Bill, Dumont made contacts among the French Canadians living in the northeastern United States. Soon they arranged for him to visit Quebec, where politicians associated with a French nationalist political party persuaded him to campaign for them. (Dumont had in 1886 received an amnesty from the Canadian government for his role in the North West Rebellion.) Quebec politics, however, did not suit Dumont, and he made his political career there brief.

FINAL YEARS

In 1888, Dumont dictated his memoirs of the 1885 Métis rebellion to B. A. T. de Montigny in Quebec City. Montigny, recorder for the city of Montreal, wrote Dumont's words in French, probably the language used by Dumont, though the Métis hero of Batoche may have thrown in some occasional Michif expressions. The illiterate Dumont provided the best first-hand account of the inner workings of the provisional government and the strategies he

In 1886, Dumont joined William "Buffalo Bill" Cody's Wild West Show in Philadelphia. Billed by Cody as "The Hero of the Halfbreed Rebellion," Dumont displayed his superb marksmanship and participated in shooting matches with legendary sharpshooter Annie Oakley.

and Riel had followed in defending Batoche. Dumont's memoir was first published in Montreal in 1889 as part of a political tract called "The Truth About the Métis Question in the Northwest."

Dumont left the province of Quebec and returned to Saskatchewan in 1890. In 1893, Dumont returned to Batoche. He built a log cabin and lived there simply.

Dumont had devoted much of his adult life to seeking justice for his Métis people. The crux of that struggle had always been land ownership rights. Possibly in 1902, Dumont finally received his own title to the land on which he had built his ferry, house, and store 30 years before.

Dumont died on May 19, 1906. Saskatchewan was now a province of Canada, having been admitted to the confederation in September 1905. Settlers were pouring into the country, transforming it into one of the most productive wheat-growing regions in the world. The western grasslands were rapidly disappearing, following the way of the buffalo. Gone with them was the way of life Dumont had known and tried to preserve. ∎

Chronology of Riel's Life

1844   born October 22 in Red River Settlement, Rupert's Land, Canada (now St. Boniface, Manitoba)

1858   travels to Montreal with fellow seminary candidates

1865   becomes clerk at law firm in Montreal

1869   leads party of Métis to force government surveying team out of Red River settlement; helps form National Committee of the Métis; sends letter to territorial governor McDougall forbidding him from entering the territory without committee's permission; Métis, led by Riel, capture Fort Garry (now Winnipeg) in November; proclaims the establishment of a provisional government based upon committee and takes over presidency

1870   carries out provisional government's execution sentence March 4 on Fort Garry prisoner, Protestant militant Thomas Scott, for insubordination; Canadian government troops put an end to the Métis revolt; Riel flees and is declared an outlaw; Manitoba Act passed by Canadian Parliament May 12, creating the province of Manitoba, as proposed and named by Riel; Manitoba enters confederation July 15

1873, 1874   elected to Canadian House of Commons but is denied seat

1875   pardoned by Canadian government under the condition he leave Canada for five years; suffers mental breakdown

1876-1878   committed to insane asylum

1880 or 1881   marries Marguerite Monet in Carroll, Montana Territory

1882   son Jean born

1883   daughter Marie Angélique born; Riel becomes U.S. citizen

1884   returns to Canada at request of Métis to lead fight for land claims in Saskatchewan country

1885   with followers takes up arms against federal troops in Saskatchewan River region; Métis are defeated and Riel surrenders; hanged for high treason by Canadian government on November 16

Louis Riel (1844–1885)

Louis Riel *(ree EHL)* is one of the most enigmatic and controversial figures in the history of Canada. To many French-speaking Canadians, he remains a hero whose defiance of the nation's federal government continues to inspire movements for cultural and even outright independence for Quebec. To other Canadians, Riel was a rebel who rightly was hanged for high treason in 1885. He is acknowledged as a founder of the province of Manitoba, which he named. However, he also was regarded by many as a madman and was, in fact, institutionalized for mental illness. As his own lawyers argued that he should be found innocent of treason on grounds of insanity, Riel stood up and claimed the opposite: it was the government of Canada, not he, that was insane. A man of deep and life-long faith, Riel nevertheless broke with the Roman Catholic Church because he believed the priests did not support the *Métis* cause. The

Métis (may TEES or *may TEE)* are people of mixed European and Indian blood. Louis Riel was not an easy man to know or to understand.

Riel led two revolutionary political movements in western Canada in the 1800's. In the first of these movements, which took place between 1869 and 1870 in the Red River settlement of what would become the province of Manitoba, he organized a government and helped craft a provisional constitution. In the second movement, which took place between 1884 and 1885 in the Saskatchewan River region of what would later become the province of Saskatchewan, Riel petitioned the federal government for extension of full democratic rights to the people of the region, which included the Métis, Indians, and economically disadvantaged white farmers. When the government failed to respond to Riel's demands for full rights, he and his followers took up arms and for a time successfully fought back the advance of federal troops into the region. In the end, the insurrection was put down, and Louis Riel was charged with and convicted of high treason.

Riel—a Métis of French and Indian origin—was brought up speaking the French language and reared in the Roman Catholic faith. He and his family had strong personal and cultural ties to what was to become the province of Quebec, the home of the majority of French Canadians. This French/Roman Catholic identity played a major role in his life, eventually making him a hero among French Canadians. The same identity made him an enemy to many English-speaking, Protestant Canadians, especially in the province of Ontario. The controversies surrounding his life, his work, and its meaning have reverberated through the years since his death and continue to affect contemporary Canada.

Chapter 1: A Métis in the Red River Settlement

ROOTS OF THE MÉTIS CULTURE

French exploration of the vast region now known as Canada began soon after 1500. Explorer Jacques Cartier made three journeys of exploration up the St. Lawrence River between 1534 and 1541, reaching as far into the interior as the present-day site of the city of Montreal, Quebec.

Later in the 1500's, French fishing vessels patrolled the east coast of present-day Canada to take advantage of the North Atlantic shoals, which teemed with fish. The fishing crews made contact with Indians who were willing to trade furs for such ordinary European-produced goods as fishhooks, kettles, and knives. A brisk fur trade soon developed. During the second half of the 1500's, felt hats covered with beaver fur grew tremendously popular in Europe. As a result, the value of Canadian beaver pelts soared, and more and more French trading ships sailed to Canada for beaver and other furs. The fur trade soon dominated European activity throughout much of the interior of North America.

English explorers, as well as the French, also plied the coastal waters of North America and probed the interior rivers and bays. In 1610, the English sea captain Henry Hudson, searching for a sea passage to Asia, sailed into an enormous body of water in northern Canada that would eventually bear his name—Hudson Bay. Later, England would use Hudson's discovery and exploration of the bay as the basis for its claim to the vast Hudson Bay region.

In 1603, King Henry IV of France and his ministers completed plans to organize the Canadian fur trade through the establishment of French colonies. In 1605, French settlers founded the colony of Acadia in what is now the province of Nova Scotia. In 1608, French explorer Samuel de Champlain founded Quebec on the St. Lawrence River. Champlain also established trading relations with the Algonquins, Hurons, and other Indian tribes in the interior. The French colonies, however, remained small and vulnerable both to the attacks of Indians by land and the English by sea.

Fur traders called coureurs de bois *("runners of the woods") established a train of trading posts between what is now the city of Montreal and the province of Saskatchewan. A* coureur de bois, *with rifle and ax, is shown in this 1891 illustration.*

In 1663, King Louis XIV of France made the struggling French colonies in Canada a royal colony named New France. The reforms carried out at this time put French settlements and colonization in northern North America on a much firmer footing, and French explorers soon began penetrating deeper and deeper into the vast interior of North America. In 1672, a new governor of New France, Louis de Buade, Comte de Frontenac, sent scouts to explore the Great Lakes, the Ohio River, and the Mississippi River. Louis Jolliet and Jacques Marquette in 1673 traveled down the Mississippi as far south as its confluence with the Arkansas River. In 1682, Rene-Robert Cavelier, Sieur de La Salle, reached the mouth of the Mississippi and claimed the entire Mississippi basin for France.

During the same period, the English established a presence in the vast region around Hudson Bay, and the Hudson's Bay Company was organized to operate fur-trading posts north of New France. English interests in the Hudson Bay region eventually would lead to years of conflict between France and England that would kindle wars on two continents.

French settlements in Canada were very different from English settlement in the 13 colonies to the south along the Atlantic Ocean seaboard. Farming was the primary economic activity in the British colonies, with frontiersmen and fur traders operating only along the fringes of settlements. French colonists also settled down and established farms, especially along the St. Lawrence River in what is now Quebec. However, the vast majority of the sparse colonial population of New France cared little for farming and pushed deep into the interior in pursuit of fur pelts that could be shipped to Europe at great profit.

In search of beavers and other fur-bearing animals, the fur traders, called *coureurs de bois (koor RUR duh BWAH)*—literally, "runners of the woods"—penetrated the immense hinterlands of North America. They established a train of trading posts between what is now the city of Montreal and the province of Saskatchewan. The coureurs also ranged south and southwest into areas that are now part of the United States. The traders learned early that to make fur trading a success they had to establish peaceful and trusting relations with the multitude of Indian communities scattered across North America. This they did, often cementing bonds through marriage with Indian women. Generations of their descendants, people of mixed French and Indian blood, would populate much of French Canada. These people of mixed blood came to be called *Métis,* meaning *mixed.*

Between 1689 and 1763, four different wars between England and France spread from Europe across the Atlantic to their colonies in North America. England (which had become part of the United Kingdom in 1707) finally triumphed in 1763 and took control of most of New France.

With the United Kingdom in control, English-speaking fur traders, already well established in the Hudson Bay country, penetrated further into the Canadian interior. These traders also married Indian women and had children, so there were English-speaking Métis as well. However, in many parts of western Canada, including the Red River region where the Riel family lived, the majority of Métis spoke French or a French creole called *Michif (MEE SHEEF),* an amalgamation of the Cree Indian language and French. Most adhered to the Roman Catholic Church. As a result, Roman Catholicism was well entrenched in the Red River settlement, and priests were numerous and widely respected there.

Métis culture also had roots in Native American cultures. Métis peoples of the plains regions continued to participate in highly organized buffalo hunts, like their Cree, Assiniboine, and Blackfoot relatives, and in general, they preferred hunting to farming. Where Métis did farm, landholding followed ancient French patterns. Landed farmers in the Red River settlement, for example, held strips—often by custom rather than title—along river banks. Interior to these riverfront plots were commons where the farmers communally held pasturing rights. These landholding traditions would become highly problematic when eastern, English-speaking settlers began to arrive, preceded by surveyors.

THE RED RIVER SETTLEMENT

The Red River—often called the Red River of the North to distinguish it from the Red River of the southern Great Plains of the United States—flows south to north through highly fertile

land shaped by Ice Age glaciers. The river marks the shared border between the states of North Dakota and Minnesota and flows 545 miles (877 kilometers) northward, emptying into Lake Winnipeg, in present-day Manitoba.

The Red River settlement, Riel's native country and that of many other Métis leaders, was by the mid-1800's the chief center of Métis culture in North America. The French Métis constituted the majority of the settlement's population, which stood at about 12,000 people in the late 1860's. French Métis settlements in the river valley tended to coalesce around Roman Catholic cathedrals and churches. As a result, many of the settlements had

Much of Riel's life as a boy revolved around the Roman Catholic Church. He was baptized at the cathedral of St. Boniface, the Riels' parish church, in what is now Winnipeg. The church burned down in 1860 but was rebuilt. Riel is buried in the churchyard.

saint's names, such as St. Boniface, home of the cathedral where Riel was baptized—and ultimately buried; St. Norbert; St. Agathe; and St. Vital, where Riel's family later took up residence.

In addition to the predominant Métis population, the Red River settlement attracted other ethnic groups during the first half of the 1800's. Beginning in 1812, Thomas Douglas, the Scottish Earl of Selkirk, a shareholder in Hudson's Bay Company, sponsored a group of Scottish emigrants to establish a colony in the valley. The colony took hold, though it remained small in comparison with Métis communities. The Selkirk settlers were centered around the village of Kildonan, which later became part of Winnipeg. Most of the Selkirk descendants remained highly attached to their Scottish heritage, including maintaining strong ties to the Presbyterian Church.

Towards mid-century, English-speaking adventurers and settlers from predominantly Protestant Ontario also began to arrive and settle in the Red River Valley. They founded Winnipeg, which would eventually become the chief city in the future Manitoba.

THE EARLY YEARS OF LOUIS RIEL

Louis Riel was born on Oct. 22, 1844, in the Red River settlement of what was then known as "Rupert's Land"—land controlled by Hudson's Bay Company (HBC) in the region that is now part of the province of Manitoba. (At the time, the Hudson's Bay Company was a British-owned, Canadian-based business firm primarily engaged in fur trading and export.) The Riel family lived in a log house on the Seine River, a tributary of the Red River, near the present-day city of Winnipeg, Manitoba.

Louis was the eldest of 11 children born to Louis Riel, Sr., and his wife, Julie Lagimodière. A pious woman who was greatly attached to the Roman Catholic Church, Lagimodière had grown up in the Red River settlement. Louis Riel, Sr., was born to the west of the Red River settlement on the plains of present-day Saskatchewan. The elder Riel's mother was part Chipewyan, an Indian nation of the northern plains. Riel, Sr., had moved with the family to Quebec (then called Lower Canada) when he was 5 years old and grew up there. As a youth, he was trained to card wool. (Carding involves separating, cleaning, and strengthening wool and other natural fibers.) Later, as a young man, he took a job with the Hudson's Bay Company. However, he was attracted to the church and left his job to enter a Roman Catholic order and study to become a priest. He later decided he did not want a vocation as a priest and returned to the Red River settlement. Soon after arriving, he met and married Lagimodière.

The Riel family was tight-knit and affectionate and scrupulous in their observance of the Roman Catholic faith. A fairly prosperous family, the Riels enjoyed some status in the large Métis community that had grown up in the Red River region by the mid-1800's. Young Louis grew up free from hardship.

The economic life of the Riel family as well as of much of the Red River settlement was dominated by the Hudson's Bay Company, which held title to the region and most of the rest of western Canada. The heart of the settlement's economy was the fur trade, which was largely—though not totally—controlled by the Hudson's Bay Company. The fur trade spurred a number of satellite industries, not least of which was the development and operation of a transportation system linking the Red

Riel's grandmother Marie Lagimodière was part Chipewyan, an Indian nation of the northern plains. She is shown with her voyageur husband, Riel's grandfather, in this 1807 illustration meeting with First Nations (the native peoples of Canada) in eastern Canada. Voyageurs were people who transported goods, especially furs, across long distances on foot or by canoe.

River settlement with the outside world. Before the coming of railroads in the second half of the 1800's, virtually all transportation and trade moved southward along the banks of the Red River into Minnesota (which became a U.S. territory in 1849 and a state in 1858), and then east by rail across the northern United States. Even transportation and communication with other parts of Canada—Ontario and Quebec, for instance—followed this same route.

One of the chief sources of jobs for Red River Métis was the haulage of goods to and from the Minnesota railhead. The wagons that made up this transportation system were known as "Red River carts." By the mid-1800's, steamships, with the power to move south against the Red's north-flowing current, also plied the river.

In 1849, when Riel was a small child, a near-rebellion among the Métis in the Red River settlement forever changed the community's economy and greatly affected Métis society. The situation also substantially molded young Riel's outlook. At issue was a court case bought against Guillaume Sayer, an independent Métis fur trader, by the mighty Hudson's Bay Company. Many western fur traders, over the course of time, had evaded the British-controlled Hudson's Bay Company monopoly by establishing independent trade with agents based in the United States to the south. Hudson's Bay Company went to court to stop this free trading. As the court prepared to rule on the case, an armed mob led by Riel's father converged on the courthouse at Fort Garry, a town that has since been absorbed into the present-day city of Winnipeg. The court found Sayer guilty but refrained from sentencing him. By not punishing Sayer, the court tacitly announced it would not enforce the Hudson's Bay Company monopoly on fur trading—effectively ending it forever.

Afterward, Métis people proudly invoked the Sayer case as a collective victory for Métis freedom. The incident had given the Métis a sense of nationhood and power. They went on to agitate for the removal of an anti-French judge, Adam Thom, from the colony's court.

Thom, a Montreal-trained lawyer of Scottish descent, had received an appointment from the Hudson's Bay Company in 1839 to establish a judicial system in the Red River settlement and serve as its first judge.

In time, Métis and Indian peoples of the Red River settlement came to believe that Judge Thom was bigoted and intolerant. He refused to use the French language in court. Several of his judgments were widely regarded in the Indian and Métis communities as unfair.

Emboldened by the Sayer case, the Red River Métis community now began a letter-writing and petitioning campaign to have Judge Thom removed from the court. The Hudson's Bay Company officials dismissed Thom as judge in 1851.

RELIGIOUS LIFE AND SCHOOLING

Much of Riel's life as a boy, and the lives of his parents and brothers and sisters, revolved around the Roman Catholic Church. The family regularly attended Mass on Sundays and services on most holy days. Religious practice was integrated into the Riels' home life, as well, with daily devotions conducted by Louis's mother, who had planned to become a nun before she married.

Louis received his early education, beginning at the age of 7, in a Catholic school in the community of St. Boniface, which also is now part of Winnipeg. A bright student who did well at his studies, Riel came to the attention of Bishop Alexandre Taché, who was an important clergyman in the local Roman Catholic establishment. When young Riel was about 14 years old, Bishop Taché arranged for him and three other local boys to go to Montreal and board at a Roman Catholic seminary, where they would study for the priesthood. To be singled out for training for the Church was a very high honor in the Red River Métis community.

THE MONTREAL YEARS

Louis and two of the other seminary candidates embarked June 1, 1858, on a five-week journey to Montreal. In what must have been a great adventure, the three boys traveled first by oxcart to St. Paul, Minnesota, a 28-day leg of the journey. In St. Paul, they boarded a steamer and sailed down the Mississippi River to Prairie du Chien, Wisconsin, where they met the railroad. By rail, they traveled east across half a continent—through Chicago and Detroit and into Canada. On July 5, they arrived in Montreal and were received at the convent of the Grey Sisters. Louis would stay in Montreal and attend the College of Montreal, the seminary which was run by the Sulpician Fathers.

In 1858, Montreal, a city with a population of more than 50,000 people, must have overwhelmed a boy from a Red River hamlet such as St. Boniface. Montreal was a national center of transportation and commerce. Like other great seaports along the Atlantic seaboard, it had absorbed great numbers of immigrants during the first half of the 1800's. This great influx from Europe resulted in the division in Montreal by ethnic areas, which also reflected the clear distribution of wealth and power.

During Riel's time in Montreal, engineers constructed a massive bridge across the St. Lawrence, which was an engineering feat upon its completion in 1859. The new bridge, christened the Victoria, for Britain's Queen Victoria, prompted the city to launch a year-long celebration. A "Crystal Palace" exhibition hall—like London's famous iron-and-glass wonder of 1851—opened in Montreal in 1860. In August of that year, Edward Albert, Prince of Wales, arrived with much fanfare to dedicate the new bridge.

SEMINARY LIFE

Life at a Roman Catholic seminary in mid-1800's Canada was highly disciplined and austere. The curriculum consisted of Latin, Greek, French, and English; science and philosophy; and theology. Riel consistently received high marks and was well regarded by his classmates. According to memoirs later written by two of his classmates, Riel was charming but could be extremely argumentative and not very tolerant of opinions in opposition to his own.

In February 1864, Riel received news that his father had died back in the Red River settlement. Young Riel was devastated, and he sank into a long depression. After a year of grief and foundering, Riel decided to leave the seminary. Like his father before him, he abandoned his goal of entering the priesthood. In March 1865, Riel left school without a degree.

Riel quickly found employment as a clerk in the law firm of Rodolphe Laflamme, a lawyer of considerable standing in Montreal.

Young Louis found the work unengaging but stayed on the job for a year. During this period, he met and fell in love with Marie Julie Guernon. She was the daughter of neighbors of the Lees, Riel's aunt and uncle who lived in Montreal. Riel and Guernon became secretly engaged in 1865 or 1866. However, when the engagement became known, Guernon's parents compelled the young girl to break with Riel. They did not hide the fact that they considered a Métis an unsuitable husband for their daughter.

Embittered, Riel left Montreal some time in 1866. Little is known about his life for the next two years beyond the fact that he spent time in Chicago and St. Paul, Minnesota, doing whatever odd jobs he could find. During this period, a momentous change took place in Canada's political life.

A NEW CANADIAN NATION

On July 1, 1867, Canada became a dominion, a united, self-governing nation. (The term *dominion* is a legal expression meaning self-governing but still a part of the British Empire.) The new federal union had a national parliament, based on the British parliamentary system, with Ottawa as its capital. Confederation, the act forming a self-governing federal union, was primarily the achievement of three politicians from Ontario and Quebec (previously designated collectively as the Province of Canada): John Macdonald, George Étienne Cartier, and George Brown.

Macdonald, known as "the father of confederation," was the dominion's first prime minister. He was a member of the Conservative Party, which he led in the pre-confederation government. Macdonald would ultimately serve longer as Canada's prime minister than any other person to the present time. He held the office from 1867 to 1873; and from 1878 to 1891.

Cartier, a Quebec politician associated with the Conservative Party, became a cabinet minister in Macdonald's government. He is largely credited with bringing Quebec into the confederation, which was no small achievement. Relations between predominantly French-speaking, Roman Catholic Quebec and predominantly English and Protestant Ontario often had been troubled. As a proponent of confederation,

Cartier believed the French language and religion would be protected by a French-controlled local government.

Brown, the third major leader of the confederation movement, was a Toronto journalist and leader of the Reform Party. Brown made important contributions to constitutional arrangements in the new dominion government, and his newspaper, the Toronto *Globe*, lobbied for confederation and for expansion of Canada across the western plains by means of construction of a transcontinental railroad. Macdonald and Cartier also envisioned a transcontinental dominion and supported the railroad plan.

Macdonald, Cartier, and Brown largely designed the new confederation at two important conferences. The first gathering, held at Charlottetown, Prince Edward Island, in September 1864, laid the groundwork for confederation among Ontario, Quebec, and the smaller Atlantic colonies, which would include Nova Scotia, New Brunswick, Prince Edward Island, and Newfoundland, if all those British colonies ultimately approved. The second conference, held in Quebec City in October of the same year, ironed out constitutional issues for the proposed confederation. After Ontario, Quebec, New Brunswick, and Nova Scotia adopted the confederation plan, the British Parliament in March 1867 passed the British North America Act, which created the Dominion of Canada, to take effect on July 1 of that year.

British Columbia, a British colony on the Pacific Coast, joined the confederation as a province in 1871. Prince Edward Island, an island off the coasts of Nova Scotia and New Brunswick, joined as a province in 1873.

Much of the groundwork for the confederation of Canada was going on while Riel was studying and working in Montreal. Rodolphe Laflamme, Riel's employer at the Laflamme law firm in 1865 and 1866, was an articulate political activist and a local leader in the anti-confederation movement. When confederation went into effect in 1867, Riel was probably somewhere in the United States. Most likely, he was aware of the happenings in his homeland, but Riel could not have foreseen the momentous changes that confederation would have on him, on his family, and on Canada's Métis community.

Chapter 2: A Leader Emerges

Riel had been away from the Red River settlement for 10 years when at the age of 24 he returned to the Red River Valley in July of 1868. Much had changed in that decade. The cathedral of St. Boniface, the Riels' parish church, had burned in 1860. A new cathedral stood in its place. Across the Red River was now the entirely new settlement of Winnipeg.

Social and cultural changes within the settlement were, however, more striking than the physical changes. An influx of people from Ontario—called "Canadians" by the local population because they favored annexation with Canada—had begun to alter the demographics of the region. For the most part, the "Canadians" were simply enterprising folk who had moved west to seek out new opportunity. A few, however, were militantly anti-Catholic and anti-French, and their intolerance seriously strained relations with the resident Métis peoples. This vocal minority had a mouthpiece in the new Winnipeg newspaper, the *Nor'Wester*. According to the editorial page of the *Nor'Wester*, residents of the Red River settlement almost universally endorsed annexation by the Canadian Confederation. Although no poll was taken at the time, the newspaper's assertions do not seem to have reflected the true opinion of the community at large.

Furthermore, the *Nor'Wester* occasionally published statements that most Métis could only regard as provocative and inflammatory. The *Nor'Wester* editors described the Métis people as "indolent" (lazy) and predicted that they would "fall back before the march of a superior intelligence"[1]—that is, before the industry and intelligence of "superior" English-speaking, Protestant Canadians.

The simmering conflict between the Canadians and the Métis was given urgency by the expected transfer of sovereignty over Rupert's Land from the Hudson's Bay Company to the federal government in Ottawa. The vast region constituted most of the western half of present-day Canada. The Métis and other Red River Valley residents were aware that Prime Minister John Macdonald and other leaders in Ottawa were in final negotiations with Hudson's Bay Company officials over terms of the sale. Macdonald was determined to acquire the land between Ontario and far-distant British Columbia and incorporate it as soon as possible into the confederation. He and many other leaders envisioned a transcontinental railroad that would bind Canada, east and west, into one transcontinental nation. Macdonald and his Cabinet members were also worried about expansionist tendencies of the United States government, a government no longer preoccupied with its own rebellion—the Civil War (1861–1865).

The impending transfer of Rupert's Land gave many of the Métis cause for serious concern. Would the acquisition of the territory by the Canadian government open the floodgates to English-speaking, Protestant settlers from Ontario and other eastern regions into the Red River Valley? Would "Canadians," with their land surveyors, push the Métis out of their houses and off their lands because they held their land by custom rather than title?

RIEL EMERGES AS A LEADER

The new federal government in Ottawa, under the leadership of Macdonald and the Conservative Party, now inflamed the highly volatile situation in the Red River settlement, though without intending to do so. Macdonald and his Cabinet, responding to crop failures in the region in 1867 and 1868 that were caused by a plague of locusts, funded a public works project designed to provide jobs and pump money into the economy. The project—the construction of a road directly connecting Ontario with the Red River settlement—had long been recommended by Simon James Dawson, a prominent Canadian civil engineer in the employ of the federal government.

Transportation between east and west still posed a major problem in the expanding new nation of Canada. All travel between settled areas of Ontario, in the southeastern corner of that province, and the Red River Valley had to be routed through the United States. The transportation network included the Red River itself, which connected the Red River settlement in the north with St. Paul, Minnesota, in the south; and the railroad across the northern United States connecting Minnesota with Detroit, which bordered Ontario.

During the summer of 1868, work was to begin on the new road, dubbed "the Dawson Road." Surveyors and work crews, composed almost entirely of English-speaking Ontarians, arrived in the Red River region and began laying out the road.

Some of the workers who arrived with the project were associated with various militant Protestant groups that preached intolerance toward French-speaking Roman Catholics. Their pronouncements and general behavior offended many in the Métis community. One of the rowdier and more vocal of the new arrivals, Thomas Scott, a man in his late 20's from Ontario, publicly proclaimed himself a member of the Ontario Orangemen. The militantly anti-Catholic group, like similar present-day organizations in Northern Ireland, was identified with the Protestant cause of William of Orange. A Dutch prince, William successfully invaded Great Britain in 1688 and defeated Catholic forces in the Battle of the Boyne in Ireland in 1690.

The federal government also ordered a general land survey in the Red River settlement during the summer of 1869, which deepened widespread Métis insecurity about land ownership. The surveying team, under the direction of Colonel John Stoughton Dennis, arrived in August. The simultaneous activities of the Dawson Road crew and the federal surveying team were to prove the catalyst for open rebellion. From this rebellion emerged a talented new Métis leader—Louis Riel.

Riel possessed passionate conviction about the Métis cause, a strong presence and speaking style, and considerable charisma. Moreover, he was well educated and spoke both French and English. Older members of the Métis community also remembered the leading role that Riel's father—Louis Riel, Sr.—had played in the Sayer case some 20 years before.

Young Riel stepped onto the public stage in August 1869 when he declared from the steps of St. Boniface Cathedral that the federally sponsored survey of land in the Red River territory posed a menace to the Métis people. His audience that day quickly realized they had a strong new leader to champion the Métis cause. Two months later, Riel proved himself a man of action when he led a party of Métis to face down the government surveying team. Confronted by Riel and his followers, the surveyors walked off the job.

In 1869, Macdonald's Cabinet announced that William McDougall would be appointed the new territorial governor (officially titled the lieutenant governor) upon the completion of the pending transfer of Rupert's Land from the Hudson's Bay Company to the federal government. McDougall was a federal official closely associated with an expansionist political party based in Ontario, and he had been responsible for ordering the Red River land survey. A strong consensus developed among the Red River Métis that McDougall should not be allowed to take up the territorial post.

TOWARD REBELLION

Métis leaders responded quickly to the Cabinet announcement. Prominent members of the community, including Riel, formed a quasi-governmental body—the National Committee of the Métis. The committee dispatched a letter, signed by Riel, to McDougall, forbidding the lieutenant governor-designate from entering the territory without the committee's permission.

The Council of Assiniboia, a Hudson's Bay Company-appointed body that was still nominally functioning as the government in the Red River region, responded by ordering Riel to appear before the council and explain his actions. In his meeting with the council on Oct. 25, 1869, Riel insisted that the National Committee of the Métis was acting in the interests of liberty and justice. He wanted to secure the common rights of all Red River residents. Riel articulated his reasoning for denying McDougall entry into the territory: because Red River residents had had no say in the lieutenant governor's appointment, McDougall had no right either to represent their interests or govern them.

Within the week, McDougall reached the border crossing at Pembina, Dakota Territory (now North Dakota), and advanced to the Hudson's Bay Company post on the Canadian side. He immediately was stopped by an armed Métis patrol. The patrol was led by Ambroise Lépine, who was soon to become Riel's chief military leader in the rebellion. McDougall had little choice but to turn back and, eventually, return to Ottawa. Riel had triumphed, at least for the moment.

Riel, backed by an armed group of about 120 Métis men, occupied Fort Garry in November. He took the fort, the chief military facility in the region, after encountering almost no opposition. As the month wore on, Riel called a series of meetings to attempt to forge a unified front with the English-speaking residents of the Red River settlement. Many of these people were disturbed by Riel's expulsion of McDougall and seizure of Fort Garry and were reluctant to be associated in any way with Riel and his rebellion. At least for the moment, Riel did not achieve unity of purpose among the various people of the valley.

THE PROVISIONAL GOVERNMENT

Meanwhile, a Canadian faction coalesced around John Christian Schultz, a local merchant. Before this group could take decisive action, a Métis patrol headed by Riel trapped and arrested Schultz and about 50 of his followers at Schultz's residence in Winnipeg. The group included Thomas Scott, the Ontario Orangeman who had arrived with the Dawson Road crew, and Charles Mair, the crew paymaster. Mair had earned himself

In December 1869, Riel proclaimed the establishment of a provisional government based largely upon the National Committee of the Métis. Riel, center, is shown surrounded by his associates in 1869.

a notorious reputation by penning a series of articles that slandered the Métis, including Métis women. Riel's patrol promptly captured Schultz and his followers, including Scott and Mair, and held them within the confines of Fort Garry.

The following day—Dec. 8, 1869—Riel proclaimed the establishment of a provisional government based largely upon the National Committee of the Métis. The committee's president, John Bruce, was named president of the provisional government. However, Riel soon took over from Bruce as president. News reached Riel later in December that the Canadian federal government had postponed the Rupert's Land transfer. Legally, nothing had changed in the settlement's official status. It still belonged to Hudson's Bay Company.

Macdonald and others in his Cabinet had postponed the transfer upon grasping the true seriousness of the situation in the Red River settlement. Macdonald then published a proclamation that promised amnesty (freedom from prosecution) for all participants in the rebellion who would immediately lay down their arms. The prime minister and his Cabinet also appointed three commissioners charged with traveling to the Red River settlement to negotiate with Riel's provisional government. The commission included Jean-Baptiste Thibault, Colonel Charles-René Léonidas d'Irumberry de Salaberry, and Donald Alexander Smith. Designated "special commissioner," Smith was the prime minister's real power-broker, and he quickly eclipsed Thibault and Salaberry. The Scottish-born Smith was head of Hudson's Bay Company eastern operations, Montreal district. Smith arrived at Fort Garry, the seat of the provisional government, in late December 1869. He began talks with Riel in early January 1870.

Smith requested and Riel agreed to a mass meeting to present the government's position. At the January 19 meeting, Smith's tone was conciliatory, and his outline of possible government concessions was well received by the crowd. In response, Riel proposed the gathering of a convention, composed equally of French-speaking and English-speaking delegates, to consider Smith's proposals. The convention assembled and began work one week later.

The convention was charged with completing and approving a "List of Rights" that could serve as the basis for a new constitution for the Red River region. Riel had probably written and published the first draft of the list in late November 1869. When members of the convention completed the final draft, it was to be submitted to the federal government in Ottawa as a basis for further negotiations.

By early February 1870, Riel's movement for rights and self-government had forged a certain amount of unity among the ethnically varied population of the Red River settlement. At the conclusion of the Smith meeting in January, the majority of the English-speaking communities of the settlement—apart from the most radical anti-Métis/anti-Catholic elements—were supporting the provisional government, and Riel quickly reorganized the government to reflect that wider base of support. Many in the community recognized that Riel's role as president was key to the success achieved thus far.

During this period, Nathaniel P. Langford, an American official with the Northern Pacific Railroad, visited Riel at Fort Garry. Langford later described his impression of the Métis leader, who was now something of a celebrity:

> Riel is about 28 years of age, has a fine physique, of active temperament, a great worker, and I think is able to endure a great deal. He is a large man . . . of very winning persuasive manners; and in his whole bearing, energy and ready decision are prominent characteristics;—and in this fact, lies his great powers—for I should not give him credit for great profundity [depth], yet he is sagacious [wise], and I think thoroughly patriotic and no less thoroughly incorruptible.[2]

THE THOMAS SCOTT AFFAIR

Riel's rule did not go unopposed. In particular, the militant Protestants who had come into the region with the Dawson Road crew were determined to undermine Riel's provisional government, if necessary, by force. Schultz and several of his followers escaped their imprisonment in Fort Garry. Later, Riel had the rest of Schultz's associates released as a gesture of good faith. It was a mistake.

One of the prisoners confined at Fort Garry was an Ontario Orangeman named Thomas Scott. In 1870, Riel's provisional government condemned Scott as a traitor and had him shot. Scott's death inflamed the people of eastern Canada against the provisional government and Riel.

Freed from captivity, Schultz, Scott, and Mair set out to gather armed partisans to launch an assault on Fort Garry. Among their recruits was Charles Boulton, an army captain and a member of the federal surveying crew that Riel had confronted the previous October. Boulton was persuaded to command the attack on the fort.

Boulton's force made its move on Feb. 17, 1870, but the men were promptly captured and imprisoned by government troops. In a subsequent provisional government trial, Boulton was condemned to death. Under pressure from Commissioner Smith and other representatives of the federal government, Riel granted Boulton clemency.

Scott, imprisoned in Fort Garry, now seemed determined to do everything in his power to inflame his guards, the court, and the provisional government. Riel decided to make an example out of Scott and charged him with insubordination. The court, presided over by Riel's assistant, Ambroise Lépine, found Scott guilty and condemned him to death.

Scott's behavior in jail—taunting and harassing his guards—could hardly be construed as a capital offense: an act deserving of the death penalty. Riel knew this but was nevertheless determined to go through with the execution, hoping that it would serve as a deterrent to like-minded individuals. Scott's death sentence was the greatest political blunder of his life. On March 4, 1870, Scott was executed by a firing squad, and his body subsequently disappeared. Some people speculated that it had been dumped into the Red River through a hole in the ice by Elzéar Goulet and Elzéar

Lagimodière because the Métis feared Scott's grave would become a shrine for Orangemen.

News of Scott's condemnation and execution provoked a firestorm of protest in Ontario, particularly among the province's Protestant majority. Rumors began to circulate as newspapers published exaggerated accounts of the events. Some of the more sensational reports claimed that the firing squad had left Scott wounded, but not killed, and that he had lain for hours in a sealed coffin, screaming, before being finished off by one of Riel's soldiers. In Toronto, a crowd of 5,000 gathered to hear Schultz denounce Riel and his associates in the provisional government, and many demanded that they all be hanged in retribution for Scott's death. The April 13 issue of the Toronto *Globe* carried a resolution penned by members of the Ontario Orangemen: "Whereas Brother Thomas Scott, a member of our Order, was cruelly murdered by the enemies of our Queen, country and religion, therefore be it resolved that . . . we, the members of the L.O.L. No. 404 call upon the Government to avenge his death, pledging ourselves to assist in rescuing Red River territory from those who have turned it over to Popery, and bring to justice the murderers of our countrymen."[3]

Newspaper editors across the province of Ontario joined the anti-Riel chorus. The editor of the *Niagara Mail* suggested that Canadian volunteers be recruited to go to the Red River settlement and "put Riel and his followers under the sod."[4] Even the generally moderate magazine, *Canadian Illustrated News,* decried Scott's execution: "The execution of Scott is a cowardly murder, and was performed in a most barbarous manner."[5]

NEGOTIATIONS WITH OTTAWA

Back in the Red River settlement itself, far from the turmoil in Ontario, Riel's provisional government and its convention wound up its constitutional work with a final draft of its List of Rights, which was readied for presentation to Macdonald's Cabinet. The List of Rights proposed the establishment of a new province, later to become Manitoba, in the Red River Valley. The province was to be created as a bilingual entity, with use of both the

French and the English languages required in the courts and at the higher levels of the provincial government. The province was to support two school systems: a public school system, mainly for the English-speaking population; and Roman Catholic schools for the French Métis, similar to the arrangement that was already functioning successfully in Quebec province. Other provisions of the List of Rights concerned public debt; authority to make treaties with the Indians; and most important, land rights. The Métis and other settlers of the region expected to have their land tenure legally confirmed.

Riel himself had suggested the name of *Manitoba* for the proposed province. It probably derives from the Algonquian (Indian) words *Manito waba*, meaning "great spirit's strait," an allusion to the waters of Lake Manitoba, which local Indians regarded as sacred.

The provisional government selected a delegation of three men to go to Ottawa, present the List of Rights to the Cabinet, and negotiate with the federal government for the people of the Red River settlement. The delegation—N. J. Ritchot, a Roman Catholic priest and a strong supporter of Riel; Judge John Black, a former Hudson's Bay Company employee; and A. H. Scott, a local businessperson—departed the settlement in March 1870 and began intensive negotiations with Macdonald's Cabinet soon after their arrival in the capital. Ritchot quickly emerged as the most capable and effective negotiator and became the leader of the delegation.

Ritchot was remarkably successful in all points but one: He was unable to obtain a written amnesty for Riel and his associates, though he was given distinct verbal assurances that Riel would receive amnesty. In his journal, Ritchot wrote: "His Excellency [Canadian Governor General Sir John Young] assured me that . . . Her Majesty was going to proclaim a general amnesty immediately, that we could set out for Manitoba, that the amnesty would arrive before us."[6]

Much of the program put forward by Riel's provisional government was actually incorporated in the Manitoba Act, which was passed by the Canadian Parliament in Ottawa on May 12, 1870. The act created the province of Manitoba, set aside 1.4 million acres

(567,000 hectares) of land for the Métis people, and sanctioned the bilingual administration of provincial government business. Manitoba officially entered the confederation on July 15, 1870.

RIEL'S FLIGHT

Macdonald's government then dispatched a military expedition to the Red River Valley under the command of Colonel Garnet Joseph Wolseley, a British officer posted to the command of British forces in Canada in 1861. Wolseley was a highly experienced commander who in 1857 had helped defeat rebels in Lucknow, a city in India, during the so-called Sepoy Mutiny, a rebellion against British rule in India.

Macdonald had insisted that the mission of Wolseley's expedition was strictly "an errand of peace." As the detachment approached the region in August, however, rumors begin to circulate that Wolseley was intent on capturing Riel. The rumors were fed by the fact that most of the force had been recruited in Ontario, a hotbed of anti-Métis and pro-Scott sentiment. Although Ritchot had attained provincial status under highly favorable conditions, he had returned to the Red River settlement in June without a written amnesty for Métis leaders.

In July, Colonel W. F. Butler, an intelligence officer assigned to Wolseley, met with Riel at Fort Garry. In a later memoir, Butler described Riel in a patronizing light, noting that the impression of Riel's authority "was not a little marred by a pair of Indian mocassins, which nowhere look more out of place than on a carpeted floor."[7] When Butler asked Riel if his provisional government intended to resist Wolseley, Riel vigorously protested: "I only wish to retain power until I can resign it to a proper Government. I have done every thing for the sake of peace, and to prevent bloodshed amongst the people of this land."[8]

The situation in the Red River settlement was greatly complicated by a matter of timing. The new, federally appointed lieutenant governor of Manitoba, Adams G. Archibald, was legally authorized to establish a new provincial government. However, given the realities of travel at the time, Archibald would not reach the Red River

Valley until after Wolseley's military expedition had arrived. Leaving Riel's provisional government in place during the brief interim would have been logical and expedient, but no legal mandate existed to do so. Wolseley, therefore, appointed Donald Smith as temporary governor until Archibald's arrival.

Riel had reason to fear Wolseley and an interim military government. Although the colonel claimed that he was on a mission of peace, his motives appeared to be anything but peaceful. In a statement made sometime after the fact, Wolseley said that he would have hanged Riel if he had caught him under arms.

Riel and his chief associates in the provisional government fled as Wolseley and his troops approached Fort Garry on Aug. 24, 1870. During a brief visit to Bishop Taché at St. Boniface before leaving the valley, Riel claimed to be satisfied with what he had accomplished: "No matter what happens now, the rights of the Métis are assured by the Manitoba Bill; it is what I wanted—my mission is finished."[9] After saying goodbye to his mother, he headed south toward the U.S. border. Once inside the United States, he settled for a time in the Métis community of St. Joseph, near Pembina, Dakota Territory.

Archibald arrived at Fort Garry on September 2 and set out to create Manitoba's new provincial government. The Nova Scotia judge and politician, fluent in French, had expressed a measure of sympathy for the Métis people. For the most part, the Métis found him a fair and capable administrator.

Riel remained in St. Joseph through fall and the winter of 1870–1871 at the urging of his friends because it would not be safe for him to return to Manitoba. In late winter, he fell ill but had recovered sufficiently by May 3 to return to St. Vital to visit his mother where she had moved after his father's death.

THE FENIAN RAID

Riel found that the situation in Manitoba remained unsettled at best. A former, disaffected associate of his, W. B. O'Donoghue, had been traveling across the United States seeking support for another armed uprising against Manitoba's new provincial government. O'Donoghue found support among the

Fenian Brotherhood of New York City. The Fenian Brotherhood, or Fenians, was a pro-Irish, anti-British organization mainly composed of Irish immigrants. Large numbers of Irish people had immigrated to the United States and Canada in the years during and after the Great Famine, Ireland's potato famine of 1845 through 1847. After the U.S. Civil War, the Fenians, many of whom were veterans of the war, organized armed forces for the purpose of striking against British interests in Canada. They had already launched raids into Quebec and Ontario as early as 1866.

To the Fenians in New York City, O'Donoghue represented the situation in Manitoba as chaotic and, therefore, highly vulnerable to Fenian attacks. O'Donoghue succeeded in recruiting a force of about 35 Fenians, and they planned to launch a raid for October 1871.

Archibald, in Manitoba, received reports of Fenian plans for the impending raid, and he called on loyal citizens to arm themselves and form companies to confront the invasion. Riel helped organize Métis companies loyal to the provincial government but did not himself serve in the militia. While reviewing Métis volunteers in St. Boniface, Archibald shook hands with Riel, an act that was widely interpreted as tacit amnesty for the former rebel. Word of the handshake soon reached Ontario, triggering another flurry of angry protests.

The Fenian raid on Manitoba fizzled. On Oct. 5, 1871, O'Donoghue's band crossed the U.S.-Canadian border and took control of a Hudson's Bay trading post on the Manitoba side. Before Archibald's forces could even reach the border, soldiers from the U.S. Army crossed the border, arrested the Fenians, and took them back to the United States.

After the very public and publicized handshake with Archibald, Riel probably thought it was finally safe to remain in Manitoba. It was not. The premier (the provincial prime minister) of Ontario, Edward Blake, responded to news of the handshake with an offer of $5,000 to anyone who would arrest or provide information leading to the arrest of "Scott's murderers." The offer, of course, referred to the man who ordered Scott's execution—Riel. A warrant for Riel's arrest was drawn up.

According to some sources, Macdonald and members of the Cabinet did not want Riel prosecuted. Putting the Métis hero on trial would only stir up Manitoba's Métis community, which for the most part had remained relatively peaceful under Archibald's rule. To avoid further troubles, the government supposedly offered money to Riel and his associate, Lépine, to get out of the country. The two men did voluntarily travel to the United States in February 1872, but it is not known whether they actually received federal money.

POLITICIAN IN THE SHADOWS

Initially, Riel lived in St. Paul, but returned to St. Joseph in June 1872. Soon, Métis friends and associates gathered around him and began urging him to run for a seat in the Canadian Parliament in general elections in September. Cooler heads warned Riel that running for a parliamentary seat would bring him national attention and expose him to serious danger. No one knew for certain how Riel would be received in Ottawa, the capital, should he be elected to the House of Commons. It was very possible that he could be arrested or even assassinated if he were to return to Ontario, where anti-French, anti-Catholic feelings continued to run high.

Riel, nevertheless, decided to run for election. He withdrew, however, not to protect himself, but to come to the aid of the French-Canadian politician George Étienne Cartier. Cartier, the political leader who had brought French-speaking Quebec into the Canadian federation, had just lost his seat in the House. (At that time, general elections were not held on the same day in every province.) Cartier, whom most Métis regarded as a friend, was a critical member of Macdonald's Cabinet, and a way had to be found for him to stay in Parliament. The seat for which Riel had intended to run, representing a largely French-speaking district in the Red River Valley, would be "safe," that is, an easy victory for Cartier. So Riel stepped aside in favor of the senior Quebec politician. (In the Canadian parliamentary system of that time, members of Parliament were not required to reside in the district which they represented in the House of Commons.)

Riel got his next chance to run for Parliament less than one year later. Cartier died suddenly in May 1873, and Riel ran in the by-election (special election) for the vacant seat and won. Ontario officials responded with yet another warrant for the arrest of Riel and Lépine in connection with the death of Scott. Lépine was taken into custody, and Riel went back into hiding.

Friends and supporters collected money to send Riel east to take his seat in Parliament. They planned to send Riel to Montreal, where he would receive additional assistance from sympathizers in that French-speaking city. Riel left Manitoba for Montreal in October 1873 and received the promised assistance upon his arrival in the city. His benefactors then arranged for Riel to travel secretly to Ottawa. Riel is believed to have made the trip, then to have turned around and returned to Montreal. It is likely that Riel rightly feared that if his presence became known to authorities, he would be arrested and tried for his role in the death of Scott.

Riel's friends in Montreal now recognized that the health of the young man—he was not yet 30 years old—had been compromised from his years of living more or less as a fugitive. At the urging of these friends, Riel went to a community run by a Roman Catholic religious order in Plattsburg, New York, to regain his health. In Plattsburg, he made the acquaintance of Fabien Barnabé, a Catholic priest in nearby Keeseville, New York. Barnabé lived with his mother and his sister Evelina in Keeseville, and the priest eventually asked Riel to become a guest in their home. The tranquil Barnabé household would become an important haven for Riel.

While in the East, Riel became aware that another general election was to be held for the Canadian Parliament in February 1874. He arranged for his friends and supporters back in Manitoba to enter his name as a candidate and campaign for him. Although Riel never set foot in Manitoba during the campaign, he again handily won a seat. This time, Riel was determined to take his rightful place in Parliament in Ottawa.

On March 30, 1874, a rumor swept through Ottawa that Riel was in the capital and was planning to try to claim his seat. The authorities dispatched platoons of police to search for Riel in the Parliament buildings and the grounds, but the police came up empty-handed.

Riel had, in fact, arrived in the capital, and he had entered the Parliament building. He even managed to sign the member's register, proof that he was there. However, the member from Manitoba once again came to the conclusion that he was, indeed, a marked man in Ontario. With his close associate, Lépine, in jail awaiting trial for the murder of Scott, Riel knew that he, too, would soon be arrested. Riel made a quick exit from Ottawa and continued the life of a fugitive.

In September 1874, Riel's supporters in Manitoba once again put his name on the ballot, and once again he was elected to represent the Métis of the Red River Valley in Canada's Parliament. However, Riel made no effort to take his seat or even to travel to Ottawa. His friend Lépine was then on trial for the murder of Scott, and Riel knew that returning to Ontario was both pointless and dangerous. (Lépine was found guilty and sentenced to death, but his sentence was eventually commuted to two years in prison by Lord Dufferin, the governor-general of Canada).

AMNESTY

Riel's long-awaited amnesty finally was granted in February 1875, but it came with a price. The politicians in Ottawa offered Riel an amnesty on the condition that he accept a banishment from Canada for a period of five years. Riel accepted their terms. Lépine was offered similar terms but refused the banishment and served the remainder of his sentence in prison.

Riel now had lived in the shadows for nearly five years. In the heady days of early 1870, he had briefly held political power and used it to great effect but had since lived as a hunted man and had endured the hatred and contempt of many of his fellow citizens. He had tried valiantly to serve his country and had been thwarted time and again. By 1875, near the breaking point, Riel despaired at another five years of banishment and what appeared to be a lack of direction and purpose in his life.

Chapter 3: Exile, Madness, and a Mission

In 1875, Riel was officially exiled from Canada, opening a bleak and disturbed period of his life. Upon exile, he spent time in the northeastern United States, where he visited friends as he wandered from place to place. Periodically, he returned to Keeseville to the haven that he had previously found with Father Barnabé and Evelina.

Demoralized and mentally and physically fragile, Riel turned more and more to religion during this period. He was, like his mother, a devout Roman Catholic who scrupulously observed the tenets of the Catholic faith. But now, intense religious devotion began to verge into *megalomania* (a mental disorder marked by delusions of great personal power or importance).

Riel claimed to have been visited by an angel, the same angel who had come to Moses on Mount Sinai. "Rise up, Louis David Riel; You have a mission to perform,"[1] Riel insisted the angel had announced to him. While attending Mass at St. Patrick's Catholic Church in Washington, D.C., in December 1875, Riel claimed to have experienced an overwhelming spiritual transformation. He later wrote that "I suddenly experienced in my heart a joy so overwhelming, that to hide my laughing countenance from the people around me, I had to open up my handkerchief and hold it in front of my face . . . . After about two minutes of these feelings of joy, I was immediately seized by a profound sadness of soul. Then it was only with great effort that I contained my sobs, cries, and tears . . . ." Riel concluded by noting that "after that, people began to treat me as a crazy person."[2] After these experiences, Riel added "David" to his name.

Riel's pronouncements and extreme behavior alarmed his friends, benefactors, and relatives, and their well-intended inquiries and gestures of friendship often triggered delusion in the man. In July 1875, Bishop Ignace Bourget of Montreal wrote Riel a letter in which he noted, "God, who has always guided and assisted you, . . . has given you a mission that you must in all respects fulfill."[3] Riel regarded the bishop's words as a divine mandate to lead and protect the Métis people of Canada.

Riel's claims and pronouncements became ever more extreme. He declared himself "the prophet, the infallible pontiff, the priest-king."[4] "When I speak," he insisted, "it is the voice of God that intones."[5] Riel also began to regard the Métis people as the chosen people, the new Israel. The Métis carried Indian blood in their veins, Riel reasoned, and now he claimed that "the Indians of North America are Jews and of purer blood than Abraham."[6]

MENTAL ILLNESS

Riel's friends grew ever more alarmed at his extreme pronouncements and increasingly bizarre and disturbing behavior. Frequent fits of ranting and weeping frightened the Barnabé family in Keeseville, Riel's nearest semblance of a family during his latest period of exile. Eventually, Barnabé was compelled to contact Riel's uncle, John Lee, in Montreal. Lee agreed to take charge of Riel and moved him into the Lee house in Montreal, an illegal act by the terms of the exile.

The move did not help. In fact, Riel's condition worsened under the care of his aunt and uncle. His fits of ranting continued, and he tore at his clothes and threatened to throw himself out of a window. At church, he interrupted a service with a fit of shouting and had to be led out of the sanctuary. Badly frightened by Riel's behavior, the family reached the end of their endurance and sought medical help for their guest.

Physicians recommended that Riel be committed to a mental asylum (hospital for the mentally ill) in Longue Pointe, Quebec. Riel was admitted to the asylum under the name of Louis R. David in March 1876. The use of an alias was necessary because he was still under the official order of banishment from Canada. In May of that year, Riel was transferred to an asylum in Beauport, a town near Quebec City. Again, he was registered under an alias, this time using the name Louis LaRochelle. Riel remained at Beauport for nearly two years.

RECOVERY

Riel's physicians at Beauport released him from the asylum in January 1878, with the advice that he lead a quiet life. Riel left Canada and made his way back to Keeseville, where once again he found compassion, acceptance, and security with Barnabé and his mother and sister. He stayed with the Barnabés for nearly a year, during which he became romantically involved with Barnabé's sister Evelina. The two became secretly engaged.

Riel, apparently cured of his mental problems and anticipating marriage, began traveling widely in the United States in an attempt to find a job that would enable him to support a family. During the long absences, Riel and Evelina exchanged letters expressing their devotion to each other.

In late 1878, Riel concluded that his destiny lay in the American West, rather than in the eastern United States. Evelina, however, was not enthusiastic about the prospect of living in the West, where American troops were still fighting Indian wars in the late 1870's. Her life in the East was comfortable, and she felt a strong sense of responsibility to her brother and aging mother. She refused to go west, and Riel refused to return east. They never saw one another again.

LIFE IN THE WEST

Riel settled in St. Joseph, Dakota Territory, in late 1878. He had lived in this Métis community for a time in 1870 and 1871, and he found it congenial. St. Joseph was close enough to Manitoba that his mother and other family members could easily visit him, and visitors from the north brought news from the province.

From such visitors, Riel learned that Manitoba had undergone a great change in the last five years. A land boom was on, and white settlers were flooding into the province. With English-speaking Protestants now constituting the majority of Manitoba's population, the Métis people feared that they would lose the concessions they had won in 1870.

In late 1879, Riel joined a band of Métis buffalo hunters and journeyed into the Milk River region of northern Montana Territory. Like the Canadian plains, the Montana region had once been French territory. It had been ceded to the United States as part of the Louisiana Purchase of 1803. Coureurs de bois had lived in the region and traded with the Indians and had, as in Canada, married Indian women. The scattered, small Métis communities of Montana were peopled with the descendants of those unions. For the next several years, Riel lived in the region, earning his keep doing a wide variety of odd jobs. He occasionally found work as an interpreter between U.S. government officials and the local Métis.

Some time around 1880 or 1881, Riel settled in the tiny community of Carroll, Montana Territory, and married a young Métis woman, Marguerite Monet. Marguerite was from a humble background and was illiterate. In 1882, she and Riel had a son, Jean. The following year, the couple had a daughter, Marie Angélique.

UNITED STATES POLITICS

In Montana Territory, Riel continued to concern himself with the welfare of the Métis people. He was troubled by the high rate of alcoholism among the Métis, and he was concerned by the toll it was taking on families and the community. Riel perceived that while the socio-economic culture of the West was changing rapidly, the Métis were not successfully adapting to a settled way of life.

Riel came to the conclusion that the typical Montana Métis man, as he saw it, had a strong passion for intoxicating drink and spent most of his earnings on whiskey. According to Riel, liquor was one of the principal causes that kept the Métis poor and, therefore, mere hunters on the prairie. If a Métis did try to settle down into the life of a merchant or farmer, the continuing use of spirituous liquors kept his purse empty, and he was likely to sink into debt that would eventually cost him his business or precious farmland.

Riel concluded that the best way to attack the alcohol problem was at the source—the traders who sold alcohol to the Métis. He brought a lawsuit against an agent of a trading company that was selling alcohol locally. He based his case on the U.S. government's prohibition of sale of alcohol to Indians living on reservations. Riel reasoned that the same law could be extended to the Métis because they were part Indian. Riel lost his case.

The case also entangled Riel in the rough partisan politics of the Montana Territory. The owner of the trading company that Riel had taken to court was a prominent member of the Democratic Party. In the 1882 territorial elections, Riel helped line up Métis support behind a Republican candidate. Although the Democratic candidate won the election, prominent local Democrats alleged that Riel had engaged in "dishonest election practices" and managed to have him charged and arrested. A court eventually threw out the case for lack of evidence.

In March 1883, Riel became a citizen of the United States. With characteristic self-aggrandizement, Riel described his naturalization as "a delightful occurrence" that "erased the border between the [Canadian] Northwest and the United States."[7]

VISIT TO MANITOBA

Riel's official banishment from Canada had expired in 1880. In June 1883, he made an extended visit to Manitoba, staying with his mother in St. Vital. During this visit, Riel gave an interview to reporters from the Winnipeg *Daily Sun*. One of the reporters noted that Riel "speaks English very well and is most particular in his choice of words." He went on to observe that Riel "has extraordinary self-possession, but when relating some stirring fact or exciting reminiscence his eyes danced and glistened in a manner that riveted attention."[8]

In the interview, Riel took the opportunity to defend his actions in the events of 1869–1870 in Manitoba.

Interviewer: *Thirteen years have passed since the troubles occurred here and time brings about wonderful changes. Now, looking at the events of that day after the lapse of thirteen years, do you now regard your action in a different light from what you did then; and if the same circumstances were to occur again, would you not act very differently?*

Louis Riel: *I am more and more convinced every day, without a single exception, I did right. Of course I don't mean to say my conduct was perfect on all occasions, because every man is liable to make trifling mistakes, but had I the same thing to go through again, I would do exactly the same. If the people of Canada only knew the grounds on which we acted and the circumstances under which we were, they would be most forward in acknowledging that I was right in the* *course I took. And I have always believed that as I have acted hon-estly, the time will come when the people of Canada will see and acknowledge it.*[9]

Some of the questions posed by the interviewer revealed much about the current political and social climate in Manitoba, where the Métis were now becoming a marginalized minority.

Interviewer: *Do you think the French language will soon be dis-pensed with here?*

Riel: *No, I scarcely believe that; at the same time successful efforts may be made to extinguish it.*

Interviewer: *Do you think the majority of the English speaking peo-ple in this country will submit to the perpetuation of two languages?*

Riel: *I do not think it would be a great burden. It may bring a little conflict, but at the same time I do not see that there is any real dis-advantage about it.*

Interviewer: *Except an inconvenience?*

Riel: *To the English, perhaps, but not to the French. Besides the con-tinuance of the French language here was made a condition of the treaty of 1870 between the provisional Government and the half-breed* [Métis] *population.*[10]

RIEL, THE TEACHER

After the St. Vital visit, Riel returned to Montana Territory, now his home. Sometime in 1883, he accepted an invitation to teach in a school at St. Peter's mission, a Jesuit outpost on the Sun River, west of the present-day city of Great Falls, Montana. (The Jesuits are a Roman Catholic order of men noted for their work in education.)

Riel worked hard and was conscientious at his teaching, but he had doubts about his effectiveness: "I am interested in the progress of the children and in the welfare of the school. I have its success at heart. And in consequence, I try to do my best. I do not know if my work is worth very much, but I do it conscientiously."[11]

The routine nature of teaching did not well suit Riel's personali-ty. He had always wanted most of all to be an actor on the public stage—to guide, persuade, and lead people. He still believed profoundly that he had a destiny and a mission, as yet unfinished, to help the Métis people.

STIRRINGS IN THE SASKATCHEWAN COUNTRY

In May 1884, a delegation of four Métis men living in the Saskatchewan River Valley was sent to Riel. Saskatchewan, west of Manitoba, was then part of Canada's Northwest Territories. The Métis committee was led by Gabriel Dumont, a widely respected trader and buffalo hunter who was known to Riel by reputation. The delegation urged Riel to come to the Saskatchewan country and help organize the Métis politically to petition the federal government in Ottawa on behalf of the citizenry.

The Dumont group and other residents of the area, Métis and non-Métis, had for years been petitioning the federal government for action on a host of grievances. These efforts had failed to yield any meaningful results. By 1884, Dumont and his associates felt they were running out of options. According to Dumont's memoirs, written some years later, the Saskatchewan River Valley Métis simultaneously came to one conclusion, "There is only one man who can help us now: Riel."[12]

All of the Métis people of Canada knew how Riel in 1870 had attained provincial status for Manitoba on a basis that was highly favorable to the Métis community. By 1884, he had acquired near-mythic status. Only Riel could achieve for the Saskatchewan Métis what he had accomplished for the Métis in Manitoba.

On May 6, 1884, the Dumont committee drew up a resolution, appending it to a draft list of their grievances toward the federal government of Canada:

> We the French and English natives of the North West, knowing that Louis Riel made a bargain with the Government of Canada in 1870, which said bargain is contained mostly in what is known as the "Manitoba Act," have thought it advisable that a delegation be sent to said Louis Riel, and have his assistance to bring all the matters referred to in the above resolutions in proper shape and form before the Government of Canada, so that our just demands be granted.[13]

In some ways, the situation in Saskatchewan in 1884 mirrored that of Manitoba 15 years earlier. The Métis were trying to preserve their unique way of life in the face of pressure from an influx of English-speaking, primarily Protestant settlers. There was one crucial difference. In 1884, the pace of change had accelerated rapidly because of the extension of the Canadian Pacific Railway across the entire width of the Canadian plains. The railroad connected Winnipeg to eastern Canada in 1881; it had reached Regina in 1882; and by 1883, it had been extended farther west to Calgary. The final spike, securing the link between British Columbia's Pacific Coast region and eastern Canada, was hammered in November 1885. The Canadian Pacific Railway opened the country's endless expanse of plains to intensive agriculture and development, and the settlers came flooding in. The arduous overland journey through the United States that Riel had traveled so often was now rendered obsolete.

The railroad and the settlers it was carrying into Saskatchewan contributed to another problem, the disappearance of the buffalo herds. The region's Indians and Métis were highly dependent on the buffalo, and the herds' extermination—accelerated by the irresponsible hunting practices of nonnative peoples—caused widespread

The Canadian Pacific Railway, completed in 1885, linked British Columbia's Pacific Coast region and eastern Canada and opened the country's expanse of plains to intensive agriculture and devlopment. With the advent of the railroad came many settlers to Saskatchewan.

privation. White settlers also were hurting, primarily from repeated crop failures and high transportation rates on the railroad. Petitions and letters begging for help had been dispatched to Ottawa, but federal officials did little or nothing.

RIEL ANSWERS THE CALL

On June 4, 1884, Riel was called out of church in Montana Territory to meet four men—Gabriel Dumont, Moise Ouellette, Michel Dumas, and James Isbister, all Métis members of the Saskatchewan delegation. Some historians indicate Riel had a premonition and may have known they had come to persuade him to return with them to Canadian territory. He later described the meeting as "Gabriel the messenger" calling back "David the prophet."[14] This was a double Biblical allusion. Gabriel was the angel who announced to Mary that she was to bear a son, Jesus; David was the great king of the Old Testament whom God treated as a beloved son.

Riel told the delegation he would give them his answer the following day. The next day, he decided he would fulfill his divine mission on the banks of the Saskatchewan. He gathered his family and their belongings and made preparations to start the long journey to the mid-Saskatchewan River Valley, almost 700 miles (1,120 kilometers) distant. At the last moment, Riel was asked to give an interview to the editor of the local Sun River newspaper, the *Sun,* to which he agreed. Riel explained that he was going to the Saskatchewan country to help the local Métis people gain their rights. Unknown to Riel, the editor taking the interview had been a 15-year-old drummer boy in Wolseley's military expedition in Manitoba in 1870, the army that was responsible for Riel's hasty flight from the province. The editor wrote that he could remember wanting to "spill his [Riel's] blood."[15]

The Riel family embarked on their long journey northward on June 10, 1884. Louis Riel was about to begin a new chapter in his life and in the lives of the people of the Canadian west.

Chapter 4: Struggles in Saskatchewan Country

Like southern Manitoba, the plains drained by the North Saskatchewan and South Saskatchewan rivers supported main-ly grassland prairie. In the eastern reaches of the Manitoba plains, rainfall was moderate, and lush tallgrass prairies thrived. In the Saskatchewan country and into present-day Alberta, climatic rainfall declined sharply, and drier, tougher shortgrass prairie predominated.

These grasslands had supported a rich ecosystem of fish, fowl, and all kinds of game. Abundant were deer, pronghorns, moose, rab-bits, coyotes, and burrowing creatures, such as prairie dogs, badg-ers, and ground squirrels. Rivers and glacial features such as kettles and sloughs scattered across the terrain as lakes and ponds harbored many waterfowl and fish species.

Central to the plains ecology and essential to the native and Métis people inhabiting these regions were the immense herds of American buffalo (bison). According to ecological historians, as many as 20 mil-lion bison once roamed the interior plains of North America. But by 1884, the buffalo had almost entirely disappeared, casualties of settled agriculture and—most notoriously—indiscriminate killing by nonna-tive hunters. The loss of the buffalo as a readily available resource was a grievous blow to Indians and Métis alike.

THE INHABITANTS

By 1884, the population of the Saskatchewan region, particu-larly the river valleys more than 100 miles (160 kilometers) north of the international boundary, had become ethnically varied and complex. For at least two centuries, native populations had been supplemented by French fur traders and subsequently the Métis offspring of the traders and their Indian wives. English-speaking populations from eastern Canada had now begun to arrive in num-bers. With the establishment of a rail line stretching all the way back to eastern Canada—finished as far as Calgary (Alberta) by 1883— many other immigrants were beginning to arrive from Europe and other parts of the world.

THE NORTHWEST TERRITORIES

Today, we think of the Canadian Northwest Territories as the arctic and subarctic lands bordering the Beaufort Sea, an arm of the Arctic Ocean, in the Far North. In 1884, however, the territories included most of the western and northern lands formerly administered by Hudson's Bay Company and previously known as "Rupert's Land"—with the exception of Manitoba in the far southeastern corner of old Rupert's Land. (Manitoba only attained its present dimensions in 1912.) Most of the territorial population, which may have numbered about 60,000, resided in the south, within several hundred miles (or kilometers) of the international border.

The capital of the Northwest Territories in the early 1880's was Battleford, a village at the fork of the North Saskatchewan and Battle rivers in west-central present-day Saskatchewan. It became the territorial capital in 1876 and would in turn be replaced by Regina, far to the south, in 1883. The executive head of the territorial government was Edgar Dewdney, the Ottawa-appointed lieutenant governor and Indian commissioner. In 1882, the Canadian federal government divided the Northwest Territories into four administrative districts: the District of Assiniboia, the District of Saskatchewan, the District of Athabaska, and the District of Alberta. Each district ranged westward from the Manitoba region to the eastern boundary of British Columbia.

Batoche, the Métis center, was in the Saskatchewan District. Most of the action of the coming North West Rebellion would take place in this district.

STRIFE FOR PLAINS INDIANS

Nothing could have proved more catastrophic for the Cree, Assiniboines, Blackfoot, and other Indian tribes of the region than the disappearance of the buffalo. These peoples' livelihoods had depended, to a high degree, on the once-plentiful plains herds. Buffalo meat provided the main staple of the Indian diet. Meat that was not eaten fresh could be dried and made into *pemmican*, a long-lasting food made by pounding dried meat, mixing it with hot fat and berries, and forming it into cakes. French fur traders quickly learned the value of pemmican, and Métis peoples depended upon it, too. Indians tanned the buffalo hides, which they used for sheathing on their shelters (usually tepees) and to make warm clothing—vital in the bitterly cold Saskatchewan winters. Indian women gathered buffalo chips (dried dung) to use as fuel.

When it became clear during the 1870's that the buffalo herds were thinning dramatically, the more forward-looking Indian chiefs concluded that their people would have to settle and adopt farming to survive. In 1876, most Indians leaders of the middle Saskatchewan region had signed Treaty Number Six with representatives of the Canadian government. The treaty stipulated that the Indian tribes would receive land on reserves (similar to reservations in the United States), cash incentives, schools, farm animals, farming tools, and food relief in times of famine. For their part, the Indians were expected to accept the surveying and sale of lands outside the reserves.

During the early 1880's, however, drought and the scarcity or disappearance of buffalo and other game brought most Indians in the region to the brink of starvation. The federal government, having promised in Treaty Number Six to provide food relief in times of famine, instead cut back on Indian relief. Some Indian leaders, especially the Cree chief Poundmaker, were trying hard to organize the Indians of the region as a unified political voice that could make itself heard in Ottawa. But the Indians never became a truly coherent political force.

THE MÉTIS OF SASKATCHEWAN COUNTRY

The Saskatchewan country had long been home to a small number of Métis; here as elsewhere, Métis people descended from unions between fur traders, mostly French-speaking, and Indian women. After Manitoba became a province in 1870, a small but steady trickle of Métis people picked up stakes and headed west, away from the new province. There were a number of reasons for this emigration. A crucial provision in the Manitoba Act, which established the province, was a set-aside 1.4 million acres

The Plains Indians' livelihood depended on the plentiful herds of buffalo that roamed the Plains. Plains Indians, such as these Cree, tanned the buffalo hides, which they used for sheathing on their tepees and to make warm clothing to protect them during the bitterly cold Saskatchewan winters.

(567,000 hectares) of land for Métis people settled in Manitoba. It had been one of Riel's greatest achievements. However, land distribution in Manitoba had not gone smoothly. It had taken the federal government nine years to sort out the claims and assign the plots. Some Métis did not have the patience to wait that long, and many were offended by homesteading regulations that seemed to favor white emigrants to, or immigrants in, Manitoba. Traditional patterns of landholding posed another problem. Métis land was held by custom rather than by deed. Métis people typically chose strips along rivers and recognized communal pasturing and hunting rights away from the river settlements. But the land allocated by the federal government, in Manitoba and elsewhere, was surveyed in squares, without regard to the natural topography of streams and rivers.

In 1873, the Métis of the Saskatchewan country, in response to the Manitoba Act, had petitioned the Ottawa government for land grants and settlement of land claims in the western regions. Eleven years later, resolution of that petition was still pending.

Some of the Métis people who had abandoned Manitoba had done so precisely because the land was being surveyed and occupied

mainly by farmers. Traditional Métis engaged in fishing and hunting—including communal buffalo hunts—and did a little farming
on the side. Their way of life occupied a middle ground between the
nomadic lifestyle of the Plains Indians and the settled way of life
practiced by the white farmers who were now infiltrating the
Canadian west. Now, the Métis worried that their unique way of
life was under threat.

Like the Plains Indians, in the early 1880's the Métis were suffering from food shortages. And like the Indians, they were not
happy with the Canadian federal government.

RIEL COMES TO SASKATCHEWAN COUNTRY

In the central Saskatchewan country, particularly the land
around the North Saskatchewan River, the white farmers were
hard-pressed as well. Like all others in the region, they had suffered crop losses from drought since 1880. Many of the settlers had
bought their land in the belief that the transcontinental railroad
would pass through the area. In the end, those tracks were laid far
to the south, on the Regina-Moose Jaw-Swift Current line in the
Assiniboia District, and land values in the Saskatchewan District
had fallen.

Many white settlers were also angry about high Canadian tar-
iffs—which made farm equipment more expensive—and high railroad rates. Farmers were highly dependent on the Canadian Pacific
Railway, because without rail transportation, they would not be
able to send their goods to eastern and international markets.

By the early 1880's, dissatisfied white settlers were organizing
for political action. In 1883, farmers formed the Manitoba and
North West Farmers' Co-operative and Protective Union for the
purpose of petitioning the federal government. Also that year, the
Settler's Union, a more radical farmers' association for political agitation, was formed. It was led by William H. Jackson.

Riel, his wife Marguerite, and their children Jean and Marie
Angélique arrived in the village of Batoche *(buh TAHSH)* in the
territorial district of Saskatchewan in July 1884. Batoche, a center of Métis settlement in Saskatchewan, was nestled on the east

side of the South Saskatchewan River about 50 miles (80 kilometers) south of the forks of the North Saskatchewan and South Saskatchewan rivers.

During their first few months in Batoche, the Riels made their home with Charles Nolin, a cousin of Riel's. Batoche would be their home for about a year; they would depend largely on the charity of Métis friends and relatives during this period.

Riel had been called to the Saskatchewan country to coordinate political action among the Métis. Soon after his arrival in July 1884, Gabriel Dumont and the other Métis leaders arranged a series of public meetings for Riel. On July 8, he addressed a Métis audience in Batoche, his first public speech in Canada since 1870.

Next, there was a large meeting at Red Deer Hill on July 11. There, several hundred people, mainly English speakers, heard Riel's speech, given in English. On July 19, he spoke to a large audience at Prince Albert, a growing trading town north of Batoche on the North Saskatchewan River. In these early speeches, Riel exercised restraint, urging a moderate approach of petitioning the federal government for redress of grievances.

Soon, Riel and Jackson struck up an alliance between the Métis and Jackson's Settler's Union. The two leaders coordinated efforts to craft a petition to Ottawa that would ideally represent the grievances of all the people in the Saskatchewan District.

Riel tried hard to draw the region's Indians—notably the Cree, Assiniboines, Stoney Sioux, and Saulteaux—into the growing coalition of petitioners. His success was limited, and his recruiting efforts among Indian tribes had an alienating effect among some white settlers. Some whites in the community were spreading rumors that Riel intended to provoke an Indian war that would bring calamity to the white settlers. It was, of course, a falsehood, but the whites' fear of Indian uprisings made them a receptive audience for rumormongering. By autumn, white opinion seemed to be shifting away from Riel. The Prince Albert newspaper *Prince Albert Times*, which had for much of 1884 taken a hard line against Ottawa, encouraging political agitation, now editorialized against Riel. Historians believe this shift occurred because Edgar Dewdney bribed the paper.

THE PETITION

Riel, Jackson, and others labored through the autumn of 1884 drafting the petition to the federal government. Finally on December 16, it was dispatched to Prime Minister John Macdonald's Cabinet in Ottawa.

It enumerated a wide range of grievances representing the interests of the Métis, Indian, and white peoples of the Saskatchewan District. One section advocated confirming land titles to all land currently occupied by Métis people. Another cited poverty and famine among the Indians and called for increases in government rations. For the white farmers, a section recommending the construction of a railroad north to Hudson Bay was included. The proposed railroad, it was theorized, would compete with the Canadian Pacific Railway and compel that company to lower its rates.

As had the Red River List of Rights nearly 15 years earlier, the Saskatchewan petition requested provincial status. The Saskatchewan District should become the province of Saskatchewan, the petition declared. Lack of representation in the governing structure had been one of the most oft-repeated grievances, and the granting of provincial status was the surest way to attain full representation and participation in the federal government.

Receipt of the petition in Ottawa was soon acknowledged by the federal secretary of state, Adolphe Chapleau. Jackson took the prompt acknowledgment as a sign that the petition would, this time, be heeded.

Now, with work on the petition finished, Riel wondered whether he should return to Montana Territory. He and his family were dependent upon Métis charity, as Riel had no means of support here. Riel, in fact, let it be known that he believed he was owed $35,000 by the federal government in Ottawa. The claim was not without foundation. Riel had been run out of Manitoba where, as a Métis, he would have been entitled to a land grant under the terms of the 1870 Manitoba Act.

Apparently, some who had reasons for wanting Riel out of the picture now seized upon his protestations of poverty. Alexis André, a Roman Catholic priest from Prince Albert, wrote Dewdney suggesting that a way be found to induce Riel to leave. "I think it is really the duty of the government to get Riel out of mischief as soon as possible . . . the presence of that man in the country will be a source of anxiety to the government, and we do not know what may happen at last."[1] André added that he believed that Riel would accept a financial inducement to leave. This initiative by a priest revealed how different Riel's relationship with the Roman Catholic clergy was to be in Saskatchewan in 1885 compared with the Red River settlement in 1869–1870.

RIEL AND THE ROMAN CATHOLIC CHURCH

As the events of the Red River Rebellion had unfolded 15 years earlier, Riel found a steadfast ally in the local Roman Catholic community. Now, local priests and bishops were highly ambivalent—when not actually hostile—toward the charismatic Métis leader. What had changed?

Riel was a man of a far different outlook than he was in 1869. He had undergone a religious transformation, followed by periods of mental instability and religious fanaticism. He had made a series of statements that the orthodox Catholic clergy could only consider wild and dangerous—advocating secession from the church in Rome and the authority of the pope and formation of a new church with a new pope in the Canadian west, for example. He had emphasized his own "divine mission," referring to himself as the "second David" who would lead the "people of Israel"—the Métis—out of their bondage.[2]

During the autumn of 1884, there were some attempts between Riel and the clergy to come to an understanding. Many of the Catholic clergy in the region were sympathetic to the Métis cause— many were French Canadians—and they ministered to the local Métis population. In September 1884, Bishop Vital Grandin of St. Albert met with Riel. Riel well understood the influence of the Catholic clergy in the Métis community and assured the bishop that he wanted the clergy's support. To attempt fence-mending, the two men agreed to form a Métis religious society, called the "Union Métisse de St. Joseph," under the auspices of Grandin. On

September 24, a special Mass was celebrated at St. Laurent to inaugurate the new society, with many Métis in attendance. Riel addressed the Métis, and proclaimed that "now we are established as a nation."[3]

The attempted alliance between the Catholic clergy and Riel turned out to be short-lived. Relations continued to deteriorate, with various members of the clergy labeling Riel a "fanatic." Riel also began discouraging his followers from attending Mass, saying that the Catholic priests were not following the law of God and only wanted to "convert the world to make money."[4] The evaporation of support among the Catholic clergy for Riel's Métis movement would prove crippling.

AN UNEASY WINTER

As January 1885 dragged into February, Riel, his Métis followers, and his supporters at large waited for a response from Macdonald's government to the December petition. No direct response ever came. Instead, the government established a commission to investigate claims for a land grant. The government had made a similar gesture after submission of the 1873 Métis petition, and nothing more had happened for over 10 years. Macdonald's commission satisfied no one.

During this period, Riel sometimes became extremely agitated and fell into fits of ranting, occasionally threatening Métis violence and retribution against almost everyone else. He began to hint darkly of a "war of extermination" against "all those who have shown themselves hostile to our rights."[5] Some witnesses to these episodes thought they saw evidence of mental instability, but to Riel's faithful followers, he remained their visionary leader.

Riel's disordered emotional state, his unconventional religious pronouncements, and his seeming turn towards violent revolution continued to erode support among whites and English-speaking Métis. More and more, his movement consisted of a dedicated Métis remnant.

Chapter 5: Riel's Rebellion

As the silence from Ottawa continued, Riel's inner circle became more impatient and agitated. Riel himself, according to Gabriel Dumont, was the first to utter the unthinkable, the prospect of taking up arms. At a gathering in late February 1885, he asserted: "They [the federal government] should at least answer us, either yes or no. And they cannot say no, since we are only asking for what has already been promised. If they don't give us our rights, we will have to rebel again."[1]

An incident at the church of St. Laurent on March 15 revealed how far things had gone with Riel—and with the clergy. From his pulpit, Father Vital Fourmond, knowing that Riel was in attendance, condemned armed resistance against the government and threatened to excommunicate (shut out from Communion and other sacraments of the church) anyone who took up arms. Riel responded from the congregation with an angry outburst. It was, in effect, his final break with the church.

On March 18, a rumor reached Batoche that a large NWMP army was approaching. Riel's Métis supporters ransacked stores in the village and arrested the local federal Indian agent, John Lash.

The next day, March 19, 1885, Riel proclaimed a provisional government with Pierre Parenteau as president. Riel was never officially part of the provisional government but was the unofficial leader. He formed a council of advisers called the *Exovedate,* a coined word derived from Latin and meaning "chosen out of the flock." Riel chose Dumont as the military commander.

The provisional government was a direct provocation to the authorities in Ottawa, who were being kept up to date on the situation in Saskatchewan District by local government officials and NWMP officials. Prime Minister John Macdonald and his Cabinet responded swiftly. Macdonald appointed Major-General Frederick Middleton as commander of government forces in the Northwest Territories. Arrangements were made to transport several thousand troops westward by rail to reinforce the NWMP forces already in place in the territory. The availability of rail transport and the presence of the NWMP in the Northwest Territories (the force had been established in 1873) were factors that had been absent in the Red River settlement in 1870, and they imposed fatal odds against Riel's political movement in the Saskatchewan country.

FIRST BATTLE

Riel's provisional government soon came under attack. A Métis force led by Dumont had occupied the village of Duck Lake, a few miles (or kilometers) west of Batoche. On March 26, an improvised government forces consisting mainly of NWMP personnel under the command of NWMP superintendent Leif Crozier approached Duck Lake. The actual government forces fell far short of the large "army" of the earlier rumor. Fighting broke out between Dumont's fighters and the NWMP forces, and a heated battle ensued. The Métis were well placed defensively and overpowered the government forces, which retreated with considerable casualties.

Dumont later related how Riel had wandered through the brush on his horse, holding a crucifix in his hand, oblivious to the extreme danger of being exposed to the gunfire all around. At the end of the battle, Riel, still holding his crucifix, ordered Dumont and his fighters not to pursue the retreating NWMP soldiers down the road to Fort Carlton, a decision that undoubtedly saved many lives.

Misfortune had hampered Crozier's forces from the start. By improperly loading the cannon the troops had with them, they rendered it useless for the duration of the battle.

Meanwhile, Indian violence against the government cropped up sporadically. The Poundmaker band ransacked and burned the village of Battleford, though that outcome had not, apparently, been the intent of Chief Poundmaker himself. At Frog Lake farther north, Big Bear's band had massacred a number of settlers in early April, though the old chief himself had tried to stop the killing.

The Indian actions complicated the situation in the territory but did little to bolster the provisional government's position. Riel's attempts to strike a common cause with the various Indian tribes had been disappointing, though Métis emissaries from his provisional government continued to talk to Indian chiefs. Some of them were telling the chiefs that Riel had supernatural powers and that he could see clearly into the future. Others spread rumors that might goad the Indian chiefs into action. One such rumor had it that Crowfoot, a widely respected Blackfoot chief based at Blackfoot Crossing (now southeastern Alberta)—and, incidentally Poundmaker's adoptive father—had joined the rebellion. The rumor was entirely unfounded.

MIDDLETON'S FIRST ASSAULT

By mid-April, General Middleton's army was advancing on Batoche, the center of Métis resistance, with a force of well over 800 soldiers. Riel and Dumont prepared to make a stand at Fish Creek, south of Batoche. As at Duck Lake, Dumont selected his positions wisely. He positioned his fighters in a wooded coulee (gulch) made by the creek's course. Then he cleverly drew Middleton's soldiers into the coulee, where the Métis fighters could take great advantage of their cover and superior positions.

In the Battle of Fish Creek on April 24, 1885, the outnumbered rebel force of 150 Métis and Indians managed to hold the ground and stop Middleton's advance. The government force, having sustained a number of casualties, retreated for the time being. With every passing day, however, Middleton gained the advantage. The railroad continued to deliver fresh troops and supplies from the east. In fact, the sponsors and builders of the Canadian Pacific Railway now regarded the federal government's rapid response to Riel's rebellion as a vindication of the tough political battles they had found necessary to wage to make the transcontinental railroad a reality.

POUNDMAKER'S VICTORY AT CUT KNIFE CREEK

The government's troubles were not over yet, however. In late April, Lieutenant-Colonel William Otter occupied the town of Battleford with a large force. Otter then turned his attention to the Poundmaker band at the Cut Knife reserve, whom he intended to punish for their pillaging of Battleford a month earlier. On May 1, 1885, Otter led a column of about 300 troops equipped with two cannons and a Gatling gun out of Battleford toward Cut Knife Creek. The column approached the Indian camp early on the morning of May 2. The Poundmaker band had only time enough to send their women and children into hiding in the surrounding brush and woods and to take up defensive positions. A six- or seven-hour battled ensued, during which Poundmaker's warriors inflicted serious casualties on the government troops. Finally, Otter had enough and withdrew.

Poundmaker's war party, despite the chief's personal misgivings and opposition, now insisted on attempting to link up with Riel's forces at Batoche. (In the Cree social structure, the peacetime chief had to yield to the war party when the band was threatened in war.) Poundmaker and his warriors now made their way eastward toward the decisive battle they expected at Batoche.

THE BATTLE FOR BATOCHE

Meanwhile, Middleton, still stalled south of Batoche, was collecting fresh troops and preparing for a decisive assault on the Métis capital and stronghold. He also armed a river steamer, the *Northcote*, and sent it northward on the South Saskatchewan River toward Batoche to attack the village from its exposed riverfront.

Middleton's 800-member force approached the southern defenses of Batoche on May 9. There, about 200 rebel fighters were preparing to defend the village. As in previous battles, they were expertly placed for defense. For three days, the fighting was intense, but by May 12, Dumont's ammunition was gone. His fighters scattered into the woods around Batoche. Middleton was now in firm control of the town.

Middleton's improvised gunboat, the *Northcote*, had proved ineffective. Attentive Métis rebels had lowered the ferry cables across the South Saskatchewan River and clipped the top of the

Canadian Major-General Frederick Middleton sent the armed river steamer the Northcote *northward on the South Saskatchewan River to attack Riel's forces at the village of Batoche. But Métis rebels lowered the ferry cables across the river and clipped the top of the boat off, disabling it.*

boat off, thoroughly disabling it. On rivers and streams in the Saskatchewan country, cables were strung from bank to bank to ferry containers back and forth. Middleton and his advisers had overlooked the ferry cables, or perhaps they knew nothing about them.

SURRENDER

Dumont and other leaders of the Métis rebellion fled, most to the United States. Riel, however, gave himself up to NWMP scouts on May 15, 1885, and was promptly taken to Middleton's headquarters. Middleton regarded Riel with a mixture of pity and contempt. He later wrote that Riel was "a mild-spoken, mild-looking man [with] an uneasy frightened look about his eyes."[2]

The Poundmaker band never made it to Batoche. In the end, Poundmaker resumed full leadership of the band when word came of Riel's defeat. Poundmaker led his warriors to Battleford to surrender to General Middleton. The surrender was received on May 26, 1885.

RIEL'S TRANSFER TO REGINA

The government in Ottawa sent orders to Middleton to have Riel transported to Winnipeg for trial, then countermanded those orders. Riel would be taken instead to Regina, the territorial capital, where there was virtually no Métis community and little sympathy for the man or his cause. Many persons sympathetic to Riel felt then—and later—that the trial's venue was a distinct liability for Riel. Had he been tried in the middle Saskatchewan country or in Manitoba, a more objective judge might have heard the case and a more sympathetic jury might have been impaneled.

Riel arrived under guard in Regina on May 23, 1885, and was taken to the NWMP barracks there to await trial. There he was imprisoned in a tiny cell and shackled with a ball and chain.

The government's charge against Riel was high treason, punishable by death. As Canada was a dominion within the British Empire—not a sovereign republic—the charge was drafted according to the ancient customs of England:

> . . . Louis Riel . . . , *not regarding the duty of allegiance, nor having the fear of God in his heart, . . . and seduced by the instigation*

of the devil as a false traitor... together with . . . divers . . . [several] false traitors . . . unknown . . . armed... with guns, rifles, pistols, bayonets, and other weapons . . . did . . . traitorously attempt and endeavor by force of arms to subvert and destroy the . . . government of this realm . . . and deprive and depose our said Lady the Queen of and from the style, honor and kingly name of the Imperial Crown of this realm, in contempt of our said Lady the Queen and her laws, to the evil example of all others in the like case offending . . . .[3]

Meanwhile, newspapers across Canada were drawing attention to the impending trial, and people were taking sides. In Quebec, where sympathy for Riel ran high, a Riel defense committee was established, which promptly engaged three prominent lawyers to defend the Métis leader. They were François-Xavier Lemieux, Charles Fitzpatrick, and James Naismith Greenshields. T. C. Johnstone, local counsel, was also part of the defense team.

Riel's lawyers studied the facts of the case and concluded that their only option to save the rebel leader's life was to plead insanity, and they built their case accordingly. This decision was not in accord with Riel's own views.

TRIAL OF THE MAD REBEL

Riel's trial for high treason opened in the Regina court on July 20, 1885. A jury of six was chosen and impaneled to hear the Riel Case. The territorial legal system provided for a 6-member jury, as opposed to the 12-member jury prescribed in the Canadian provinces. All of the jurists were English speakers and Protestant—none French Canadian, Métis, or Roman Catholic.

When the court began hearing the case on July 28, the courtroom was packed with spectators, eager to see the "mad rebel." Officiating from the bench was Judge Hugh Richardson, an appointee of former Canadian Prime Minister Alexander Mackenzie's administration. Much of the court's testimony would be given in French, but Richardson was not bilingual. The judge and jury depended on translators for much of the testimony.

The prosecution was represented by five prominent attorneys: George Wheelock Burbidge, Christopher Robinson, Thomas Chase

Casgrain, Britton Bath Osler, and David Lynch Scott. The defense lawyers Fitzpatrick, Lemieux, and Greenshields were also present to make their case for Riel.

Lawyers for the prosecution opened their case. They called their star witness, Charles Nolin, to the stand. Nolin was the Riel cousin with whom Riel, his wife, and their children had stayed in Batoche after arriving from Montana Territory in July 1884 and for several months thereafter. During the height of the rebellion, Riel's Exovedate council had arrested Nolin as an informant. Riel himself probably pardoned and freed his cousin.

Nolin made a number of charges against Riel, many of them personal and unsubstantiated. Riel's intent, Nolin went on to allege, had been to break up Canada into a number of separate countries, each to be governed by a distinct ethnic group. Riel had passed himself off as a prophet, Nolin said, deceiving and manipulating his simple, uneducated Métis followers in attempting to carry out this treasonous program. Nolin was suspected of being paid by government officials for his testimony, but the allegation has never been proved.

Drawing upon the testimony of a number of other Crown (state) witnesses, the prosecution made much of Riel's orders to take up arms against the government and his wild threats to carry out a war of extermination. They seized upon his contention that the federal government owed him substantial amounts of money, and tried to show that Riel had acted out of self-seeking, mercenary motives. There were also allegations that Riel had attempted to incite an Indian war against the white settlers of Saskatchewan.

The defense team had lined up witnesses to bolster Riel's insanity plea. Riel was deeply troubled by the allegation that he was insane, but he had little choice but to go along with the legal team that the Quebec benefactors had provided him. In open court, however, Riel complained:

> I cannot abandon my dignity. Here I have to defend myself against the accusation of high treason, or I have to consent to the animal life of an asylum. I don't much care about animal life if I am not allowed to carry with it the moral existence of an intellectual being.[4]

In court, the defense lawyers called Fathers André and Fourmond to testify. Father Fourmond described how easily Riel could slip into an agitated, irrational state of mind:

> *In private conversation, he was affable, polite, pleasant, and charitable to me. I noticed that even when he was quietly talked to about the affairs of politics and government, and he was not contradicted, he was quite rational; but as soon as he was contradicted on these subjects, then he became a different man and would be carried away with his feelings.[5]*

Other witnesses for the defense described Riel's outbursts of temper and his fits of ranting.

The star defense witness was Dr. François Roy, superintendent of the asylum in Beauport, Quebec, where Riel had been confined for mental illness in 1876–1878. Dr. Roy stated his professional opinion that Riel was suffering from megalomania.

The prosecution then called a series of medical doctors to refute Roy's testimony of insanity. With varying degrees of certainty upon cross-examination, the doctors testified to Riel's sanity. The debate about Riel's mental state continues to this day.

Finally, attorney Fitzpatrick, leader of the defense team, gave an impassioned defense of Riel's actions. According to observers in the courtroom, it had a profound effect on many present, including jurors.

Fitzpatrick began by recounting briefly the history of the Métis people in the territory and describing their grievances in a sympathetic way. He also took pains to commend the government soldiers who had put themselves in harm's way to put down the rebellion. The bulk of Fitzpatrick's address was a summation of the evidence that supported the defense's assertion that Riel was not sane and therefore not responsible for his actions.

After the Fitzpatrick summation, Judge Richardson gave Riel the opportunity to address the court. He spoke for more than an hour, in measured tones, choosing his words, in English, carefully.

> *For 15 years, I have been neglecting myself . . . . My wife and my children are without means, while I am working more than any representative of the North-West. Although I am simply a guest of*

this country [by then, Riel was, in fact, a U.S. citizen] . . . , *I worked to better the conditions of the people of the Saskatchewan at the risk of my life . . . . I have never had any pay . . . .*[6]

I was working in Manitoba first . . . to get free institutions for Manitoba; they have those institutions to-day in Manitoba, and they try to improve them, while myself, I who obtained them, I am forgotten as if I was dead . . . . Manitoba, when the Government at Ottawa was not willing to inaugurate it at the proper time, I have worked till the inauguration should take place, and that is why I have been banished for five years . . . .[7]

Even if I was going to be sentenced by you, gentlemen of the jury, I have the satisfaction if I die—that if I die I will not be reputed by all men as insane, as a lunatic . . . .[8]

If you take the plea of the defence that I am not responsible for my acts, acquit me completely since I have been quarreling with an insane and irresponsible Government. If you pronounce in favor of the Crown, which contends that I am responsible, acquit me all the same. You are perfectly justified in declaring that having my reason and sound mind, I have acted reasonably and in self-defence, while the Government, my accuser, being irresponsible, and consequently insane, cannot but have acted wrong, and if high treason there is it must be on its side and not my part.[9]

Observers then and later have thought that Riel's speech, rational and well-reasoned, may have discredited the insanity plea and sealed his doom.

THE VERDICT

Now the leader of the prosecution, attorney Robinson, summed up the prosecution's case. He disputed the defense's assertion of Riel's insanity and repeated the allegation that Riel had, all the while, acted out of selfish, carefully calculated motives. Robinson suggested that the defense was based on incompatible premises—that Riel was insane and that he was at the same time a passionate patriot. The defense team, he stated, should have made a choice between their defenses. "They cannot claim for their client," he insisted, "what is called a niche in the temple of fame and at the same time assert that he is entitled to a place in a lunatic asylum." Robinson summed up with the opinion that Riel was "neither a patriot nor a lunatic."[10]

Richardson next gave the charge to the jury. He stated that the evidence suggested that the accused was, indeed, sane, and that the evidence of Riel's guilt was overwhelming.

The jury deliberated for an hour and returned their verdict: guilty. The jury foreman, speaking for all the jurors, recommended mercy in sentencing.

Richardson was under great pressure to impose the death sentence. The federal bureaucracy had taken pains to ensure a hostile venue and court for Riel's trial, and the judge must have realized—if indeed, he wasn't explicitly informed—that the politicians in Ottawa wanted Riel out of the way. After giving Riel a second chance to speak to the court—Riel again spoke at length—Richardson pronounced a sentence of death by hanging. The execution was to be carried out in Regina on September 18, about six weeks hence.

Several of the jurors later said that the jury had been faced with a dreadful decision: to find Riel insane, which they could not accept, based on the evidence; or to convict him of a capital offense, while not wanting to see him executed. Under these circumstances, the members of the jury opted for the guilty verdict with the mercy plea, probably realizing that it would make little difference in the end.

Meanwhile, the government was meting out justice to scores of westerners accused of participating in the rebellion. A number of Riel's followers (those not successful in escaping) were tried and found guilty of treason-felony, a lesser offense than high treason and not a capital crime. Riel's associate and collaborator in the petitioning movement, William H. Jackson, was tried but acquitted by reason of insanity. The Indian chiefs Poundmaker and Big Bear were tried and convicted according to the treason-felony statute and sentenced to prison terms. Eleven Indians, Crees and Assiniboines, were convicted of murder for their participation in the April 1885 Frog Lake killings. Three had their sentences commuted (reduced) to prison terms. The remaining eight would be hanged at Battleford on Nov. 27, 1885.

RIEL AWAITS HIS FATE

As news of the death sentence imposed on Riel spread throughout Canada, the rest of North America, and the world, pleas for clemency (mercy) poured in to the government in Ottawa. Within Canada, opinion was sharply divided between English-speaking, Protestant, and French-speaking, Catholic, regions. The Orangemen and other militant Protestants of Ontario called for the government to carry out the death sentence, while many French-speaking citizens of Quebec demanded that the sentence be commuted.

On September 17, one day before his scheduled execution, Riel was informed that the date was being postponed so that his case could be appealed to the territorial appeals court in Manitoba and the Privy Council in London. In the end, both these courts rejected the appeal. Now Macdonald's Cabinet was in a difficult position. If they let the execution go forward, there would be an outcry from Quebec. If they commuted it, Ontario would be in an uproar. The Cabinet decided to convene a panel of three doctors of high reputation to re-examine Riel and make a secret report to them. Ultimately, two of the doctors concurred with the prosecution in Riel's trial that Riel was sane; the third doctor, Dr. François-Xavier Valade of Ottawa, concluded that Riel was unable to distinguish between right and wrong on political and religious subjects. A consensus of the panel was good enough for the prime minister and the majority of his Cabinet; the execution order would stand.

In July 1885, Riel (standing in prisoner's box) was tried for high treason in a Regina courtroom. All of the jurors were English-speaking Protestants. Many observers thought that Riel's impassioned but rational speech may have discredited the insanity plea and sealed his doom.

A MARTYRED REBEL

The government now rescheduled Riel's execution for Nov. 16, 1885. In the dark, early-morning hours of that day, Riel wrote his final letter to his mother, wife, and children in Manitoba. "It is two hours past midnight," he wrote. "Good Father André told me this morning to hold myself ready for tomorrow. I listen to him, I obey. I am prepared for everything . . . . But the Lord is helping me to maintain a peaceful and calm spirit . . . .

I am doing everything I can think of to be ready for any eventuality, keeping myself in an even calm . . . . Yesterday and today I have prayed God to strengthen you and grant you all his gentle comfort so that your heart may not be troubled by pain and anxiety."[11]

Riel spent the rest of this final night in prayer with Father André. The morning of November 16 dawned clear and chilly. Riel received extreme unction, the Catholic rite for the dying, at 7 o'clock. Shortly after 8 o'clock, guards led the condemned man out from his cell and to a door leading to the scaffold. After a final round of prayers, Riel said to Father André and the other priest in attendance:

> *I thank God for having given me the strength to die well. I am on the threshold of eternity and I do not want to turn back. I die at peace with God and man, and I thank all those who have helped me in my misfortunes.*[12]

The executioner bound Riel's hands and led him to the scaffold. Riel declared that he forgave all his enemies and asked their forgiveness in turn.

Riel saw that Father André was weeping and said, "Courage, Father."[13] The executioner pulled a white hood over Riel's head, stepped back, and sprang the trap. Riel died almost instantly.

BURIAL

Four weeks later, authorities sent a coffin containing Riel's body in a guarded boxcar to St. Boniface, Manitoba. There, in the cathedral that was so much a part of his youth and early adulthood, Riel would be mourned and honored. The Requiem Mass (Catholic funeral service) for Riel was held Dec. 12, 1885. In attendance were Riel's mother, his wife, Marguerite, his children Jean and Marie Angélique, and many others who had known and loved him. Riel's remains were buried in the cemetery of the cathedral, today within the city limits of Winnipeg.

Riel's story was to have a final sad footnote. His wife, Marguerite, died in St. Vital, Manitoba, in May 1886. Both of the Riel children were to die young: daughter Marie Angélique in her teens of diphtheria; and son Jean in his 20's in an accident.

A NEW WORLD: THE CANADIAN
PRAIRIE ROVINCES

Louis Riel had dedicated his life to the establishment of a unique place and identity in Canada for his Métis people, but in the end, the Indians and Métis of the west were overwhelmed by advancing settlement. This trend accelerated after the completion of the Canadian Pacific Railway in November 1885.

Within a decade or two after Riel's death, the Canadian west was transformed beyond all recognition, from the Métis point of view. Saskatchewan and Alberta were finally admitted into the Canadian Confederation as provinces in 1905. These lands, like those in Manitoba, were subjected to intensive agriculture, and the Canadian prairies became one of the primary wheat-producing regions of the world. The provinces eventually supported other industries as well, notably oil and gas production. By 1911, Saskatchewan had a population of almost 500,000. Alberta in that census year registered a population of about 375,000. Both provinces would grow far more populous as the 1900's progressed. The patterns of settlement and land use that became established in the Canadian west left no room for the Métis lifestyle of an earlier age.

RIEL'S LEGACY

Perhaps no single figure has generated as much controversy in Canada as Louis Riel. Partisans have viewed him as a deluded, vengeful rebel, deserving of death; or alternately, as a martyr to democratic ideals.

The trial and execution of Riel had immediate consequences in Quebec. Voters there turned to a Quebec nationalist party in provincial elections in 1886. Nationally, the strength of Macdonald's Conservative Party ebbed, paving the way for Canada to elect its first French-speaking prime minister, Wilfrid Laurier of the Liberal Party, in 1896.

Indeed, Riel's legacy reverberated into the mid-1900's and beyond, as French separatists in Quebec gained power in the 1960's, 1970's, and 1980's. In the provincial referendum of October 1995, they came very near to separating the province from the rest of Canada.

In a 2005 ceremony to commemorate the 120th anniversary of Riel's death, a procession was led from St. Boniface Basilica to the rebel's gravesite in Winnipeg.

Pierre Elliott Trudeau, a French Canadian and Canada's prime minister from 1968 to 1984, invoked Riel's legacy in a different way. He sought to secure rights for French-speaking Canadians within a more democratic, pluralistic Canada, even as he fought against Quebec separatism. In 1969, under Trudeau's leadership, the Canadian Parliament passed the Official Languages Act. This law requires Canadian courts and other government agencies to provide services both in French and in English.

In a visit to the Saskatchewan legislature in Regina in 1968, Trudeau expressed his view that Riel had resorted to armed rebellion because the governmental establishment had turned a deaf ear to him:

This setting . . . makes me think of how difficult it is for us to understand Louis Riel. What forces motivated this man? What social conditions led him to believe that nothing short of rebellion would serve the cause to which he had pledged himself? How many other Riels exist in Canada, beyond the fringe of accepted conduct, driven to believe that this country offers no answers to their needs and no solutions to their problems?[14]

Since the mid-1900's, many other Canadians—of varied cultural heritages—have considered and re-evaluated the extraordinary career of Louis Riel. At the 100-year anniversary of Riel's death in 1985, the Canada Council (now the Social Sciences and Humanities Research Council of Canada) published a five-volume, bilingual edition of Riel's works, *The Collected Writings of Louis Riel*. It was a unique honor: up to that time, no other Canadian had been so published in a complete edition. In 1992, the Canadian Parliament formally recognized Riel's crucial role in the 1870 founding of Manitoba, another indication of the rehabilitation of his reputation.

In Riel's interview for the *Winnipeg Daily Sun* in 1883, the Métis leader had stated his belief that the time would come when Canadians would see and acknowledge that he had acted honestly. Louis Riel's tragedy is that the recognition came a century too late. ∎

Poundmaker (1842–1886)

Poundmaker was perhaps the most influential Indian leader of the Canadian western plains—the present-day provinces of Manitoba, Saskatchewan, and Alberta—during the years in which these regions were opened to large numbers of nonnative settlers. Canada became an independent, unified nation in 1867 when the eastern provinces of New Brunswick, Nova Scotia, Ontario, and Quebec formed the Dominion of Canada. Soon thereafter, land-hungry residents of those eastern provinces, the United States, and such European areas as the United Kingdom, Germany, the Netherlands, Poland, Scandinavia, and Ukraine turned their attention to the fertile northern plains of North America. In the process, ways of life based upon hunting and gathering were overwhelmed by agriculture and other forms of industry. Long before 1900, the buffalo herds on which the Plains Indians had chiefly depended were gone and all Indians of the region had been moved to reserves (called *reservations* in the United States).

During this brief, tumultuous period, Poundmaker attempted to preserve the well-being of his people while acting as peacemaker in conflicts with the Canadian government and settlers. Though not entirely successful in either endeavor, Poundmaker attained the stature of a wise and revered leader.

LIFE ON THE CANADIAN PLAINS

The land we now call "the prairie provinces" had for centuries provided abundantly for its sparsely scattered inhabitants. Through the mid-1800's, the land supported communities of native hunter-gatherers including the Cree, Assiniboine, Saulteaux, Stoney Sioux, Blackfoot, Piegan, Blood, and Sarcee tribes. It also supported scattered communities of mixed-race people called the *Métis (may TEES* or *may TEE)*. These were largely descendants of male French fur traders and Indian women. Most Métis communities retained French language and culture, including Roman Catholicism, but their way of life was not entirely unlike that of the surrounding Indian peoples. Like the Indians, they favored hunting over farming, also relying on the rich game resources of the region.

To see the interior plains of North America today is to see an ecosystem so entirely transformed by intensive agriculture that the presettlement grasslands are almost unimaginable. A century and a half ago, however, the native grassland ecosystem remained largely intact on the Canadian plains.

It stretched from moisture-nourished tallgrass prairies in the east (present-day Manitoba) to tougher, drier stands of shortgrass to the west (Alberta and southwestern Saskatchewan). Scattered through the prairies were isolated stands of aspens, birch, and Manitoba maple, as well as rare outcroppings of rugged, hilly terrain, especially toward the west. The rich ecosystem supported deer, pronghorns, moose (in the more northerly places), rabbits, coyotes, and all kinds of burrowing creatures, such as prairie dogs, badgers, and ground squirrels. The air flocked with birds of all kinds; streams and lakes teemed with fish. Glacial depressions such as kettles and sloughs scattered uncounted thousands of lakes and ponds across the terrain, homes for ducks, grebes, geese, and other water birds.

But above all else, there were the immense herds of American buffalo (bison). Before the full

Poundmaker was a Cree Indian. He was adopted as a young man by Crowfoot, a Blackfoot chief. Poundmaker became a Cree chief as an adult. Cree Indians live in Canada and in Montana in the United States. Blackfoot or Blackfeet (as they are called in the United States) lived on the Great Plains of the United States and Canada. Today, they live on a reservation in Montana and on three Canadian reserves.

force of nonnative settlers descended upon the grasslands during the 1800's, as many as 20 million bison roamed the interior plains of North America, according to some estimates. The buffalo were the mainstay of the people of the Canadian plains—both Indian and Métis. This vital and irreplaceable resource would disappear during Poundmaker's lifetime.

A CREE YOUTH

Poundmaker was born into a Cree family of considerable status in the Battleford region of present-day Saskatchewan, probably in 1842. His given Cree name was Pitikwahanapiwiyin. His father, an Assiniboine (a tribe closely allied to the Cree) was a *shaman* (a person regarding as having supernatural powers), a person of high rank. His mother, who was of mixed French-Canadian and Indian blood, was sister to a Cree chief.

Poundmaker's youth was not an easy one. His father died when Poundmaker and his brother were young children. His mother took them to live with members of the Red Pheasant band of Cree, people related to her. Shortly thereafter, his mother died and Poundmaker and his brother remained with the Red Pheasant band. The band made its home in the vicinity of the Eagle Hills, south of today's city of Battleford, Saskatchewan.

As was expected of Cree boys, Poundmaker participated in the frequent buffalo hunts mounted by his band. It was the Cree's primary economic and food-gathering activity. The Cree employed very specific, well-honed methods for trapping buffalo herds. They built corrals called *pounds* and then drove the animals into the nearly closed circles, trapping them. Once snared, the beasts were easy to slaughter with either bows and arrows or guns, which the Cree obtained through trade networks. Poundmaker became an expert pound builder and buffalo hunter. Thus he acquired, at some time in his youth, the name Poundmaker.

Another fundamental of Cree life was the tribe's enmity toward the Blackfoot tribe and confederated tribes—the Piegan, Blood, and Sarcee—who inhabited areas to the west and south (present-day Alberta). The Cree had about a century earlier emerged from woodlands to the east and north to contest grassland territory—prime buffalo hunting ground. The Cree had displaced the Blackfoot and related tribes to the west. Fighting between the groups was a common feature of Plains life in the future prairie provinces.

Amid the bounty of the Plains ecology and the intricate social networks of Indian tribes and Métis, Poundmaker grew into his maturity. He acquired stature as a superb hunter and a wise, thoughtful leader in tribal councils. Contemporaries described him as "tall and good looking, slightly built and with an intelligent face, in which a large Roman nose [is] prominent."[1] They also noted his dignified bearing and fine speaking skills.

DAILY LIFE AMONG THE CREE

Sometime in the early 1870's, Poundmaker married Little Beaver, daughter of a warrior in the Red Pheasant band. (Later, he would also marry Little Beaver's sister, Grass Woman. Little Beaver delivered their first son, Sakamo-tana, in 1873 or 1874. Little Beaver would eventually give birth to a daughter and another son. Grass Woman would give birth to a daughter.

Life for Poundmaker's Red Pheasant band followed traditional and seasonal patterns. A great deal of daily life centered around food gathering and preparation, especially all aspects of buffalo hunting and processing. Buffalo hunting was a highly organized and communal activity. Hunting and fishing for other game, on the other hand, were less structured. Hunters occasionally brought in deer, antelope, rabbits, gophers, prairie chickens, ducks, and geese to supplement buffalo meat. Weirs (fencelike barriers) were built in fast-running streams to trap fish. Women and children gathered eggs, Saskatoon berries (sweet, red bush berries), and Indian turnips, edible tubers that provided a staple of the diet.

Marriage and children were central to Cree life. Men of high rank typically had two or more wives. In addition to child rearing, women performed most of the labor associated with the necessities of daily life. Except for hunting, which was the prerogative of men, women gathered food, cooked it, preserved it, and stored it. After buffalo hunting, women butchered the carcasses. They then tanned the

The Cree built corrals called pounds, *then drove buffalo into them, trapping the animals. Poundmaker acquired his name as a youth because of his expertise in building these corrals. This illustration shows a Cree buffalo pound near Fort Carlton, Saskatechewan.*

hides, which provided clothing and sheathing for shelters. Women also gathered buffalo chips (dried dung) for use as fuel. Cree life was also enriched by a wide range of sacred observances. Associated with many of these were ceremonial dances, often in lively gatherings. Gift giving was an important part of such events. Those of high rank, especially chiefs, were expected to give generously. At other times, Cree people enjoyed a wide range of lively games. Some games were strictly segregated by sex; others were open to all.

BORN A CREE, EMBRACED AS A BLACKFOOT

In 1873, when Poundmaker was about 30 years old, an event without precedent in Plains native society changed his life and the political landscape of the Plains region. That year, the Blackfoot chief Crowfoot spied Poundmaker in a truce meeting with the Cree and noted his striking similarity to his own lost son, killed in battle. Crowfoot resolved to adopt Poundmaker, though a Cree, as his own son. Poundmaker agreed to go with Crowfoot to his settlement at Blackfoot Crossing near the fork of the South Saskatchewan and

In 1873, the Blackfoot chief Crowfoot, impressed with Poundmaker's peacekeeping efforts with the Cree and striking similarity to his own son, who was killed in battle, adopted Poundmaker as his own son.

Bow rivers in present-day southeastern Alberta. There he received a Blackfoot name, Makoyi-koh-kin (Wolf Thin Legs) and embraced his newfound status as Crowfoot's son. When Poundmaker returned to the Cree after visiting Blackfoot Crossing, his status as Crowfoot's son and the wealth in horses he received from his new family increased his status with the Cree band. The two men remained deeply attached for the rest of their lives. As time went on, they discovered they had many similarities. Above all, both were pragmatists and peacemakers.

TREATY MAKING

In 1870, the government of newly confederated Canada annexed Manitoba as a province. Canadian leaders based in Ottawa, notably Prime Minister John Macdonald, were laying plans in 1871 for a transcontinental railroad to tie the new Pacific coast province of British Columbia to the east and open the way for settlement of the Plains. Establishing treaties with the native peoples of the Plains region became a high priority of the federal government in Ottawa.

Such Indian leaders as Poundmaker and Crowfoot were aware of the intentions of eastern Canadians to expand into the Plains region. These leaders saw that the buffalo herds were already thinning dramatically because of settlers' expansion westward. Reluctantly, the Indian leaders resolved to negotiate with the Canadians for the best terms they might obtain.

In the summer of 1876, Indians of the middle Saskatchewan River region assembled at Fort Carlton on the North Saskatchewan River to negotiate a treaty with Alexander Morris, governor of the Northwest Territories (which then included what is now Saskatchewan and Alberta), and other agents of the Canadian government. The fort had been an important fur-trading post in the days when the Hudson's

Bay Company (HBC) owned the vast interior region of the future Canadian prairie provinces, but it was now primarily an administrative post for the Canadian government, which had purchased the interior territories from HBC in 1870.

Present at the 1876 treaty gathering were a number of Assiniboine and Cree leaders, including Mistowasis, Atukukoop, Beardy, and Poundmaker. Notably absent was Big Bear, a senior and much-respected chief. His exclusion would cast a shadow over the Indians' future relations with Ottawa.

The Canadian government offered Treaty Number Six: In return for the Indians' agreement to move onto reserves, the Indians would be given the reserve land, some cash incentives, schools, farm animals, and farming tools. The negotiations dragged on for several days, much to the irritation of Governor Morris, as the Indian leaders debated among themselves. Poundmaker proved the most skeptical of the leaders. He understood the immense challenge that conversion to settled farming life posed, and wanted to ensure that the native peoples would not be abandoned to desperate circumstances. At Poundmaker's insistence, the Canadian authorities were compelled to promise food rations in case of famine. At last, the Indian representatives in attendance consented to the treaty. Poundmaker, still doubtful of the government's stated intent to help and protect the Indians, nonetheless signed on Aug. 23, 1876.

When Chief Big Bear learned of the signing of the treaty, he asked what promises had been made to protect the buffalo and whether the treaty banned capital punishment for Indians. He was far from satisfied with the answers he received and refused to sign.

CHIEF POUNDMAKER

In the years following Treaty Number Six, Poundmaker came into his own as a mature leader. In 1878, he and followers broke away from the Red Pheasant band of Cree and formed their own band, with Poundmaker recognized as chief. The next year, the Poundmaker band chose their reserve, according to treaty provisions, in the vicinity of Cut Knife Hill along the Battle River—just to the west of Battleford and near the present-day border between Saskatchewan and Alberta.

These were challenging times for the new chief and the Indian peoples of the Canadian prairies. The buffalo herds were disappearing with astonishing rapidity. Their annihilation was partly due to the encroachment of settlement and partly the result of unrestrained, reckless hunting by nonnative people. As the take from each hunting expedition decreased, the Cree and other tribes of the region began to experience famine. Even the secondary game—deer, antelope, rabbits, prairie chickens—was growing scarcer.

Chief Poundmaker was determined that the members of his band should learn how to farm properly to ensure their survival and ultimate prosperity. According to commitments made in Treaty Number Six, the federal government had provided farming instructors to the Indians. Poundmaker worked hard to master the techniques demonstrated by the farming instructor. The results, however, were disheartening. Crop failures followed. Like many white and Métis neighbors, Poundmaker's band was learning that farming in a marginal climate is difficult at best. The full development of agriculture in Saskatchewan would await dry farming techniques (growing crops without irrigation), introduced some years later.

To make matters worse, the federal government prohibited Indians on the reserves from selling the grain they grew; they were to use it as food for themselves only. At the same time, government officials provided no means for the Indians to grind their grain into usable flour. Poundmaker repeatedly submitted requests for a gristmill to the government's Indian agents, but to no avail.

At the same time, the Cree and other Indians were attempting to make another difficult transition: that of living in and building log houses rather than tepees sheathed in buffalo hides. The wooden structures, though warmer, became smokehouses because the Indians did not know how to build proper chimneys. Whereas tepees were made of flexible material and featured flaps one could open to let in fresh air, the wooden houses were dark and stuffy. The Indian women found log houses harder to keep clean than tepees.

Insects and mice thrived in the log houses. This had never been a problem in tepees, for the women could simply open them up and brush the tepees out—even disassemble them—when necessary.

Another destabilizing force was the migration of numbers of Lakota Sioux into the Saskatchewan country after the 1876 massacre of General George Custer's force at Little Big Horn and the U.S. retribution that followed. The Lakota Sioux represented increased competition for the dwindling herds of buffalo and other scarce food resources. Among the Sioux was Chief Sitting Bull, one of the two great victors of the Battle of Little Big Horn (the other being Crazy Horse). By late 1876, however, Sitting Bull and his people were in retreat and facing desperate conditions. Scattered groups of Sioux crossed the border in late 1876. Sitting Bull remained on the Canadian side until the summer of 1881. Poundmaker met the old warrior in the summer of 1880 and learned of the terrible suffering of Sitting Bull's Lakota Sioux from famine during the previous winter.

FAMILY TIES, A GOVERNOR-GENERAL'S GUIDE

In the summer of 1881, Little Beaver's sister—sister-in-law to Poundmaker—married Robert Jefferson, the white school teacher on the Red Pheasant reserve. To some observers, the marriage seemed symbolic of the increasing interweaving of Indians' and nonnatives' lives and destinies. But to others, particularly white settlers in the nearby town of Battleford, the union was scandalous.

Also in 1881, the Marquis of Lorne, son-in-law to Queen Victoria (through his marriage to Princess Louise) and governor-general of Canada, made a tour of the Northwest (prairie) Territories. According to the confederation constitution, the governor-general serves as the Crown's (British king's or queen's) representative in Canada. Poundmaker, as a well-known and respected Indian leader of the region, was asked to serve as guide for the governor-general's progress through the rough Saskatchewan country to a final destination at the city of Calgary (in the present-day province of Alberta). He readily agreed.

Poundmaker persuaded the government officials to change the projected route so as to pass through Blackfoot Crossing, the home of Chief Crowfoot, his adopted Blackfoot father. The governor-general genially received Poundmaker and Crowfoot and expressed admiration of their apparent leadership and wisdom.

Sometime in late 1881, Poundmaker decided to send his eldest son, Sakamo-tana, who was about 8 years old, to a boarding school run by Roman Catholic priests in Duck Lake, about 115 miles (185 kilometers) to the east. It was a painful decision for Poundmaker and his family, especially for Little Beaver, the boy's mother. Yet Poundmaker believed that the changes coming to the Saskatchewan country would require new kinds of training, which schooling might provide.

THE POLITICAL LEADER

Through the early 1880's, game continued to dwindle, crops continued to fail, and the buffalo all but vanished. Each successive winter became a time of starvation for Indians in the Northwest Territories. Bands formerly well fed and healthy looking became emaciated. Clothes became tattered and shabby now that the chief source of Indian clothing, buffalo hide, was unattainable. Malnutrition and disease claimed many Indian victims.

Things became so desperate that even stubborn Chief Big Bear consented in 1883 to accept settlement on a reserve. His band took up residence on a reserve near Frog Lake, north of the North Saskatchewan River. But the chief, his followers, and many other Indians in the region seethed with anger and frustration.

All the while, Poundmaker was emerging as a political leader of all the Indian peoples of the Saskatchewan country. He traveled from reserve to reserve, talking to chiefs, in an effort to encourage the Indian peoples to present a united front to government authorities and lobby for just and fair treatment.

A terrible blow came in early 1884. The government announced that because of cost-cutting pressures, the budget for Indian services was to be reduced. Most ominously, food rations were to be curtailed to the Indians of the Saskatchewan country, who were already starving and desperate. The decision was made apparently in violation of the federal government's obligations according to Treaty Number Six, which pledged food aid in time of famine.

A SEASON OF STRIFE

By 1884, widespread desperation among the Indians of the Saskatchewan country coupled with failure of the Canadian government to meet its treaty obligations toward them set the stage for conflict. Disaffection was widespread among Métis communities as well, who had their own long list of grievances with the Canadian government.

The conflict that would become the North West Rebellion began with a series of scattered incidents. In June 1884, Poundmaker's reserve hosted a gathering of several thousand area Indians to hold a Thirst Dance, a major religious ceremony among the tribes to reaffirm their faith in the sun spirit. During the gathering, an Indian was accused of assaulting John Craig, a government Indian agent supervising a food storehouse on an adjacent reserve. As a result, a large contingent of North West Mounted Police (NWMP) entered the Poundmaker Reserve and demanded that the chiefs turn over the accused man. Poundmaker and Chief Big Bear, in attendance at the ceremony, refused to violate the sanctity of the ceremony by complying. The accused man later gave himself up and was tried and sentenced to one week in jail.

Meanwhile, the Métis community resolved to call on a seasoned and charismatic leader, Louis Riel. After leading uprisings against the Canadian government in Manitoba in 1869–1870, Riel had been banished to the United States. He had eventually settled in

Poundmaker emerged as a political leader of all the Indian people of Saskatchewan country. He is shown in this 1885 illustration on horseback, addressing his men at the Cut Knife reserve in Saskatchewan.

Montana Territory, just below the Canadian border. Métis representatives went to meet Riel there in June 1884 and persuaded him to return to Batoche *(buh TAHSH)*, a Métis community on the South Saskatchewan River in central present-day Saskatchewan. Thus by late 1884, two potential resistance leaders emerged in the region: Poundmaker among the Indians and Louis Riel among the Métis.

The year 1884 wound to a close with the peoples of the Saskatchewan country facing their most desperate winter yet, and no relief in sight from Ottawa.

THE NORTH WEST REBELLION

In 1885, as Indian and Métis peoples emerged from yet another winter of desperate privation and frustration, they prepared to use means more forceful than just talks.

On March 19, 1885, Riel formed a provisional government and gathered an army at Batoche. Pierre Parenteau was named president and Gabriel Dumont his army commander. This was a direct provocation to the authorities in Ottawa, who swiftly arranged to transport several thousand troops westward by rail to reinforce the NWMP forces already in place.

The first confrontation came a few days later. A Métis force led by Dumont occupied the village of Duck Lake. On March 26, an improvised government force consisting mainly of NWMP personnel and led by NWMP superintendent Leif Crozier approached Dumont's force at Duck Lake. Fighting broke out and a heated battle ensued. The Métis were well placed defensively and overpowered the government force, which retreated with considerable casualties. Riel gave an order to allow the government personnel to retreat without pursuit, which probably saved them.

ATTACKS ON BATTLEFORD AND FROG LAKE

Meanwhile, Poundmaker led a group of Cree to Battleford to seek out the Indian agent there and request extra food rations. Though the agent refused to receive the Indian leader, Poundmaker was able to meet with the

Indian agent. As he attempted to make the case with the agent for increased food rations, some members of Poundmaker's party broke into and looted homes and stores in the village. Poundmaker had lost control of his followers. Fortunately, residents of the village had previously withdrawn to a nearby fort for protection. The next morning, the Indians withdrew and returned to the Cut Knife reserve.

The month of April brought more armed clashes. Big Bear's band, the most reluctant of all Saskatchewan Indians to enter into a treaty with the federal government, now acted out years of grievances and suffering. The Indians left their reserve and wandered into the nearby settlement of Frog Lake, killing nine, including a priest and a government official. The old chief's pleas to stop the violence and killing had failed to deter his more warlike younger warriors.

The failures of both Poundmaker and Big Bear to avert unnecessary violence stemmed from the social structure within Cree communities. In times of peace, Cree chiefs led effectively by their powers of persuasion. In wartime, however, war chiefs appropriated the decision-making power. At both Battleford and Frog Lake, Poundmaker and Big Bear were overruled by their war chiefs, who tended to be younger, more aggressive members of the community.

THE BATTLE OF FISH CREEK

The Frog Lake warriors moved on to Fort Pitt to the west. There on April 14–15, they besieged the fort and forced the small NWMP force there to flee down the North Saskatchewan River.

By mid-April, Major-General Frederick Middleton, chief commander of the government forces in the North West Rebellion, was advancing on Batoche, the center of Riel's Métis resistance, with a force of 800 soldiers. Riel and his commander, Dumont, prepared to make a stand at Fish Creek, on the east side of the South Saskatchewan River, to the south of Batoche. As at Duck Lake, Dumont selected his positions wisely. In the Battle of Fish Creek on April 24, the outnumbered rebel force of 150 Métis and Indians was able to hold the ground and stop Middleton's advance. The government troops, having suffered heavy casualties, retreated to recover and regroup.

A COMMON ENEMY

Meanwhile, Riel's provisional government worked frantically to try to enlist the scattered Indian belligerents in a concerted resistance against the rapidly growing government forces. Riel sent emissaries to a number of important Indian chiefs, including Poundmaker and Crowfoot. Both of these leaders held back from joining Riel's provisional government. Though the Indians and Métis now had a common enemy, their objectives were not identical. The Indian leaders also seem to have distrusted Riel, a charismatic, quasi-religious leader whom they may have regarded as not entirely rational. Poundmaker expressed his doubts about Riel to Robert Jefferson, his brother-in-law, who was now the government's farming instructor on the Cut Knife reserve.

Under pressure from his warrior camp, Poundmaker in late April signed a communication to Riel which cautiously offered encouragement to the Métis leader. Though the letter apparently did not reflect Poundmaker's true sentiments, it would be used against him at his government trial some months later.

CONFRONTATION AT CUT KNIFE

By late April, Lieutenant-Colonel William Otter had taken the town of Battleford with a large force. Otter then turned his attention to Poundmaker's Cut Knife reserve. He intended to punish the Poundmaker band for their pillaging of Battleford a month earlier. On May 1, 1885, Otter led a column of about 300 troops equipped with two cannons and a Gatling gun (an early machine gun) out of Battleford toward the Cut Knife reserve.

As the column approached early in the morning of May 2, the Poundmaker band had only enough advance warning for the women and children to hide in surrounding brush and woods and for the warriors to take defensive cover. Nonetheless, they inflicted serious casualties on Otter's force, and after a six-hour pitched battle, Otter

In early May 1885, Canadian Lieutenant-Colonel William Otter led a column of about 300 troops equipped with two cannons and a Gatling gun out of Battleford toward Poundmaker's Cut Knife reserve. The Poundmaker band inflicted serious casualties on Otter's force and, after a six-hour battle, Otter withdrew.

withdrew. The Indian warriors might have pursued Otter's force had Poundmaker not intervened. Some military historians believe that the Poundmaker band might have annihilated Otter's force had they pursued them.

BATTLE AT BATOCHE

Meanwhile, Middleton, still stalled south of Batoche, was collecting fresh troops and preparing for a decisive assault on the Métis provisional capital and stronghold. He also outfitted a river steamer, the *Northcote*, as a gunboat, and sent it northward on the South Saskatchewan River toward Batoche.

Middleton's army of 800 troops approached the southern defenses of Batoche on May 9. In and around the town were roughly 200 rebel fighters. The rebels were expertly placed for defensive action, but Middleton's overwhelming force of numbers was not to be deterred this time. The battle raged on for several days, ending in the decisive defeat of the rebels and the capture of Batoche by May 12. Middleton's improvised gunboat, the *Northcote*, had never even weighed in. Attentive Métis rebels had lowered the ferry cables across the South Saskatchewan River and clipped the top of the boat off, thoroughly disabling it. On rivers and streams in the Saskatchewan country, cables were strung from bank to bank to ferry containers and even passenger cabins back and forth. Middleton and his advisors had not taken the ferry cables into account.

SURRENDER AT BATTLEFORD

The rebel defeat at Batoche was, in effect, the end of the North West Rebellion. Riel soon gave himself up to Middleton, and Dumont and other Métis leaders fled southward across the boundary with the United States.

Despite Poundmaker's opposition and misgivings, the Cut Knife war party had attempted to link up with some of Riel's Métis supporters. When news of the fall of Batoche became known, however, Poundmaker resumed full leadership of the band. Poundmaker realized that further resistance would be useless. He made sure a group of teamsters (people who haul things with a team of horses) who had been captured while driving government supply wagons through the Eagle Hills were protected. Earlier, the chief had intervened to save the men's lives when Indian warriors and Métis rebels threatened to kill them.

On May 26, 1885, Poundmaker and his followers gave themselves up to Middleton at Battleford. The leaders among them were immediately imprisoned.

POUNDMAKER'S TRIAL

The Canadian federal government moved quickly to bring the North West rebels to justice. In early July 1885, Poundmaker was taken under guard to Regina, a town in southern Saskatchewan made the territorial capital in 1883.

Poundmaker's trial, on a charge of treason-felony, began in Regina on August 17 with Judge Hugh Richardson presiding. Louis Cochin, a Roman Catholic priest who had long been a friend of the Cree chief, testified on Poundmaker's behalf. The courtroom was filled with spectators representing the federal and territorial bureaucracy, as well as the social elite of Regina. Only the trial of Riel, concluded a few weeks before, had attracted more interest.

Poundmaker was deeply disheartened to learn that Robert Jefferson, his brother-in-law and farming instructor on his reserve, was a witness for the prosecution. The letter Poundmaker's warriors had written to Riel at the height of the rebellion, bearing Poundmaker's mark, was important government evidence, and Jefferson testified that Poundmaker had indeed made his mark on the document.

The defense built much of its case on the many instances in which the Cree chief had intervened to prevent or curtail violence, such as when he prevented the warriors in his band from pursuing Colonel Otter's badly beaten soldiers at Cut Knife in early May or the protection he gave to the captured teamsters. Poundmaker himself made this point on the witness stand: "Everything I could do was done to stop bloodshed."[2]

After a brief deliberation, the jury returned a guilty verdict. Judge Richardson imposed a sentence of three years' imprisonment in the Stony Mountain Penitentiary north of Winnipeg, Manitoba. Unlike high treason, the lesser charge of treason-felony did not require mandatory capital punishment.

In 1885, Poundmaker (in striped blanket) was taken under guard to the territorial capital of Regina to stand trial on a charge of treason-felony.

Soon after the trial, Northwest Territories Lieutenant-Governor Edgar Dewdney visited Poundmaker in his cell. Dewdney, well known to the Cree chief, asked Poundmaker to write his adoptive father, Crowfoot, and urge him to remain on his Blackfoot Crossing reserve and refrain from any hostile action. Rumors reaching the lieutenant-governor had suggested that the Blackfoot leader might take up arms to avenge Poundmaker's capture and sentencing. In return, Poundmaker asked a favor of Dewdney. He requested that he be allowed to keep his long hair in prison. Poundmaker had long, thick hair, which he groomed and braided fastidiously.

Dewdney promised to convey his wishes to the prison authorities. It was the only concession made to the Cree chief, and he did, in the end, keep his long hair. Poundmaker, in return, agreed to send the requested communication to Crowfoot.

Meanwhile, state retribution against Indian participants in the rebellion followed its course. On November 27, eight warriors, Cree and Assiniboine, were hanged at Battleford. They had been convicted of murder by the courts.

IMPRISONMENT

In the late summer of 1885, a train chugged its way eastward from Regina to Winnipeg. That train carried Poundmaker, now a national celebrity, to a waiting wagon that would take him up the Red River Valley to the Stony Mountain Penitentiary. There Poundmaker expected to serve out his three-year sentence.

Although the penitentiary was new and well furnished and the food adequate, Poundmaker aged, lost weight, and suffered bouts of depression. For a Cree who had always enjoyed a great measure of freedom and intense closeness to the land, imprisonment was a dreadful ordeal. Unknown to the Cree chief, however, a number of people on the outside were making efforts to get him released before the end of his sentence. Among these advocates were members of the Roman Catholic clergy, friends of Poundmaker, and some members of the press. In early March of 1886, Poundmaker was released and sent back to the Cut Knife reserve in the Saskatchewan country.

FINAL DAYS

All was not well when Poundmaker returned to the Cut Knife reserve in March 1886. He learned that his second wife, Grass Woman, had gone off with another man, a terrible personal blow. Little Beaver and Poundmaker's younger children were waiting for him, however. The chief was appalled to see the destitute state of his family and band members. In the harsh aftermath of the rebellion, gangs of scavengers had raided the Indian reserves, looting and vandalizing. The Cree of Cut Knife would continue to endure hardship for some time to come.

Poundmaker tried to concentrate on the future. He took another wife, Stony Woman. And he made plans to visit Crowfoot, whom he had not seen since before the rebellion. Settled Indian peoples now had to apply for permission from government agents to leave their reserves. So he went to Battleford and made the appropriate arrangements.

In May 1886, Poundmaker and Stony Woman started out on foot to Blackfoot Crossing. That spring brought cold, rainy weather, causing Poundmaker to suffer a severe sore throat. The couple made it to Crowfoot's compound in Blackfoot Crossing but, by then, Poundmaker was seriously ill with a high fever. Though he rallied for a time, Poundmaker collapsed and died on July 4, 1886. He was in his mid-40's, prematurely aged by hardship.

Poundmaker was buried where he died, at Blackfoot Crossing (later known as Gleason, Alberta). About 80 years later, in 1967, Poundmaker's descendants returned his remains to Cut Knife Hill, which had been home to the Cree chief for most of his later years.

Today, many people regard Poundmaker as an ideal leader, a chief who always sought the well-being of his people while advocating peaceful methods. Though he did not achieve most of his aims, his ideals continue to inspire Native Americans today. ■

Notes

GABRIEL DUMONT

1. Peter Charlebois, *The Life of Louis Riel* (Toronto: New Canada Publications, 1975) 127.
2. Gabriel Dumont, *Gabriel Dumont Speaks,* trans. Michael Barnholden (Vancouver: Talonbooks, 1993) 44.
3. Dumont 45-46.
4. Dumont 48.
5. Dumont 57.
6. Dumont 71.
7. Dumont 23.

LOUIS RIEL

Chapter 2

1. Hartwell Bowsfield, ed., *Louis Riel: The Rebel and the Hero* (Toronto: Oxford University Press, 1971) 28.
2. "Riel, Louis," *Dictionary of Canadian Biography, Vol. XI: 1881 to 1890,* 1982.
3. "Scott, Thomas," *Dictionary of Canadian Biography, Vol. IX: 1861 to 1870,* 1976.
4. Sean Sullivan, "Canadian Illustrated News and the Red River Rebellion (October 1869–August 1870)," *Library and Archives Canada.* 19 January 2004 <http://www.collectionscanada.ca/cin/026019-204-e.html>
5. Sullivan.
6. "Riel, Louis."
7. W. F. Butler, *The Great Lone Land: A Narrative of Travel and Adventure in the North-West of America* (London: Sampson Low, Marston & Company Limited, 1872), *The Project Gutenberg EBook #15401,* 18 Mar. 2005 <http://www.gutenberg.org/files/15401/15401-8.txt>
8. Butler.
9. "Riel, Louis."

Chapter 3

1. *Montreal Daily Star* 22 Aug. 1885, qtd. in Thomas Flanagan, *Louis "David" Riel: Prophet of the New World* (Toronto: University of Toronto Press, 1979) 51.
2. Louis Riel, *The Collected Writings of Louis Riel.* Gen. ed. George F. G. Stanley, 5 vols. (Edmonton: University of Alberta Press, 1985) 2: 163-164.
3. Albert Braz, *The False Traitor: Louis Riel in Canadian Culture* (Toronto: University of Toronto Press, 2003) 30.
4. Riel 2: 73,75.
5. Riel 4: 146
6. Riel 2: 39.
7. Riel 3: 307.
8. *Winnipeg Daily Sun,* 29 June 1883, qtd. in Riel 2: 422.
9. *Winnipeg Daily Sun,* 29 June 1883, qtd. in Riel 2: 414-415.
10. *Winnipeg Daily Sun,* 29 June 1883, qtd. in Riel 2: 414.
11. Bowsfield 91-92.
12. Gabriel Dumont, *Gabriel Dumont Speaks,* trans. Michael Barnholden (Vancouver: Talonbouis, 1993) 40.
13. Peter Charlebois, *The Life of Louis Riel* (Toronto: New Canada Publications, 1975) 127.
14. Braz 32.
15. Bowsfield 104.

Chapter 4

1. Bowsfield 113-114.
2. Braz 33.
3. Maggie Siggins, *Riel: A Life of Revolution* (Toronto: Harper Collins Publishers Ltd., 1994) 358-359.
4. Dumont 26.
5. Riel 3: 54, 56.

Chapter 5

1. Dumont 45-46.
2. Bowsfield 133-134.
3. Louis Riel, *The Queen v. Louis Riel.* Introduction by Desmond Morton (Toronto: University of Toronto Press, 1974) 3-4.
4. *The Queen v. Louis Riel.* 212.
5. *The Queen v. Louis Riel.* 240.
6. *The Queen v. Louis Riel.* 324.
7. *The Queen v. Louis Riel.* 314.
8. *The Queen v. Louis Riel.* 316.
9. *The Queen v. Louis Riel.* 324.
10. *The Queen v. Louis Riel.* 326-327.
11. Bowsfield 148-150.
12. Bowsfield 150.
13. Bowsfield 150-151.
14. Braz 7.

POUNDMAKER

1. "Pitikwahanapiwiyin (Poundmaker)," *Dictionary of Canadian Biography, Vol. XI: 1881 to 1890,* 1982.
2. *Dictionary of Canadian Biography.*

Recommended Reading

BOOKS

Barnett, Donald C. *Poundmaker*. Don Mills, ON: Fitzhenry & Whiteside, 1976.

Braz, Albert Raimundo. *The False Traitor: Louis Riel in Canadian Culture*. Toronto: Univ. of Toronto Pr., 2003.

Brown, Chester. *Louis Riel: A Comic-Strip Biography*. Montreal: Drawn and Quarterly, 2003.

Dumont, Gabriel. *Gabriel Dumont Speaks*. Trans. Michael Barnholden. Vancouver: Talon Bks., 1993.

Flanagan, Thomas, ed. *The Diaries of Louis Riel*. Edmonton: Hurtig, 1976.

—. *Louis "David" Riel: Prophet of the New World*. Rev. ed. Toronto: Univ. of Toronto Pr., 1996.

—. *Riel and the Rebellion: 1885 Reconsidered*. 2nd ed. Toronto: Univ. of Toronto Pr., 2000.

Giraud, Marcel. *The Métis in the Canadian West*. 2 vols. Lincoln: Univ. of Neb. Pr., 1986.

Howard, Joseph Kinsey. *Strange Empire: A Narrative of the Northwest*. 1952. St. Paul: Minn. Hist. Soc., 1994.

Jenish, D'Arcy. *Indian Fall: The Last Great Days of the Plains Cree and the Blackfoot Confederacy*. Toronto: Viking Penguin, 1999.

Klerks, Cat. *The Incredible Adventures of Louis Riel: Canada's Famous Revolutionary*. Canmore, AB: Altitude, 2004.

Peterson, Jacqueline, and Jennifer S. H. Brown, eds. *The New Peoples: Being and Becoming Métis in North America*. Lincoln: Univ. of Neb. Pr., 1985.

Quan, Holly. *Native Chiefs and Famous Métis: Leadership and Bravery in the Canadian West*. Canmore, AB: Altitude, 2003.

Siggins, Maggie. *Riel: A Life of Revolution*. Toronto: HarperCollins, 1994.

Sluman, Norma. *Poundmaker*. Toronto: Ryerson, 1967.

Woodcock, George. *Gabriel Dumont: The Métis Chief and His Lost World*. Orchard Park: Broadview, 2003.

WEB SITES

Canadian Heroes Fact or Fiction. <http://www.collectionscanada.ca>

The Canadian Museum of Civilization. <http://www.civilization.ca>

Histor!ca. The Historica Foundation of Canada. <http://www.histori.ca>

"The Northwest Resistance." *The University of Saskatchewan Library*. <http://library.usask.ca/north-west/contents.html>

"Gabriel Dumont." "Poundmaker." *Virtual Saskatchewan*. <http://www.virtualsk.com/current_issue>

Glossary

amnesty *(AM nuh stee)* a general pardon or conditional offer of pardon for past offenses against a government.

bison *(BY suhn or BY zuhn)* a wild ox of North America, the male of which has a big, shaggy head and strong front legs; buffalo. Bison have a large hump and short, thick, curved horns.

Blackfoot a member of a tribe of American Indians that formerly lived in the northwestern United States and southern Canada and now live on reservations in Montana and Alberta, Canada. The Blackfoot speak an Algonkian language. Blackfoot are called Blackfeet in the United States.

clemency *(KLEHM uhn see)* gentleness in the use of power or authority; mercy or leniency.

Confederation *(kuhn FEHD uh RAY shuhn)* the union of Ontario, Quebec, Nova Scotia, and New Brunswick in 1867, joined since then by six other Canadian provinces.

coureur de bois *(koo RERR duh BWAH)* a wandering woodsman, hunter, and trader in the early French settlements in Canada and adjoining parts of North America. Literally in French "runner of the woods."

Cree a member of a tribe of American Indians living in Montana and in central and southern Canada. The Cree form a number of bands that speak various dialects of a single Algonkian language.

dominion *(duh MIHN yuhn)* a self-governing territory that is a part of the British Empire.

Fenian *(FEE nee uhn or FEEN yuhn)* a member of the Fenian Brotherhood, an Irish secret organization founded in the United States about 1858 for the purpose of overthrowing English rule in Ireland.

House of Commons the lower house of the Parliament of Great Britain and Northern Ireland, or of Canada, composed of elected representatives.

megalomania *(MEHG uh loh MAY nee uh)* a mental disorder marked by delusions of great personal power, importance, or wealth. It is associated with schizophrenia and other disorders.

Métis *(may TEES or may TEE)* people of mixed white and American Indian ancestry. Métis culture developed primarily in the Red River Colony (in present-day Manitoba) in the 1800's.

Michif *(MEE SHEEF)* a hybrid language derived from French and the language of the Cree Indians.

Orangeman a member of a secret society formed in the north of Ireland in 1795 to uphold the Protestant religion and Protestant control in Ireland.

Parliament *(PAHR luh muhnt)* the national lawmaking body of Canada, consisting of the Senate and the House of Commons.

pemmican *(PEHM uh kuhn)* dried lean meat pounded into a paste with melted fat and pressed into cakes. Pemmican was an important food among certain tribes of North American Indians.

pound an enclosure for keeping, confining, or trapping animals.

premier *(prih MIHR or PREE mee uhr)* a prime minister; chief officer.

prime minister the chief minister in certain governments, who is the head of the cabinet and the chief executive of the government.

reserve an area of land set aside and reserved by the Canadian government for American Indians as a permanent tribal homeland. Called a *reservation* in the United States.

shaman *(SHAH muhn or SHAM uhn)* a priest with magic powers, as over diseases or evil spirits.

tepee *(TEE pee)* a tent of the North American Indians, especially the Great Plains, formed of bark, mats, or animal skins stretched over poles arranged in the shape of a cone.

treason *(TREE zuhn)* the action of being false to one's country or ruler. Helping the enemies of one's country is treason.

voyageur *(VWAH yah ZHERR)* a French Canadian or person of mixed race who worked for the early fur trading companies transporting men and supplies to and from remote places, especially by canoe through unsettled regions.

Index

Page numbers in *italic* type refer to pictures.